# TENNIS
## KEEP IT SIMPLE

Donald D. Klotz

*University of Iowa (retired)*

Edited by
Steve Wilkinson
*Gustavus Adolphus College*
and
Jane Latourette

**Championship Books**
**A Division of Wm. C. Brown Publishers**
2460 Kerper Boulevard
Dubuque, Iowa 52001

Cover photo by Bob Coyle
Text illustrations by Lan Vu

Library of Congress Catalog Card Number: 88-70751

ISBN 0-697-08483-3

Printed in the United States of America by Wm. C. Brown Publishers
2460 Kerper Boulevard, Dubuque, IA 52001

10  9  8  7  6  5  4  3

# TABLE OF CONTENTS

**Keep It Simple** captures the essence of Dr. Don Klotz, a gifted tennis instructor and philosopher of life, now 81 years old and well beyond his official retirement. The familiar acronym "KISS" includes the word "stupid." However, a more appropriate final word for Dr. Klotz is "smarty." He always discovers brilliance in any apparently uncoordinated youngster who wants to play tennis. Dr. Klotz marvels at the wonderful computer that rests on each of our shoulders. He delights in showing each of his students how good they already are, without his assistance. Therefore, "Keep It Simple, Smarty" is clearly the best way to use the acronym "KISS."

"Keep It Simple" is the basic philosophy of Dr. Klotz's "Volley Method" of teaching tennis. Instruction begins at the net, where the distance over the net is the shortest, and moves progressively to the baseline. "Never teach two things at once. . . Don't over-teach. . . There is so much the beginner already knows. . . Volleying is like catching. . . Just keep it simple."

The sections in this book come from his own writings, kept as mimeographed handout sheets, and found in Dr. Klotz's file cabinets and closets. Most originally appeared in a different form as articles in WORLD TENNIS between 1950 and 1980. Jane Latourette and I have edited them considerably, changing even the titles, and we have organized them into six primary chapters. Lan Vu has brought animation and life to the pages with his fine illustrations.

The succession of the six main chapters reflects Dr. Klotz's approach to tennis. "Keep It Simple" and "Follow the Volley Method," the first two chapters, have been mentioned already. "Improve Concentration" and "Develop Strategy," the next two chapters, reflect the special emphasis that Dr. Klotz puts on these two traditional tennis topics. "Refine Your Strokes," the next chapter, typically dominates most books on tennis. However, Dr. Klotz disavows classic form, having seen many great players use a variety of styles. Finally, Dr. Klotz does emphasize "Practice Effectively," the final chapter. Here, the emphasis is on practicing **as you intend to play**.

**Keep It Simple** is a valuable tool for the tennis player, coach or pro. Although many of Dr. Klorz's original articles were written up to thirty years ago, the wisdom of his simplicity is very current. The book avoids the traditional arguments on form, thereby enhancing its adaptability to a wide variety of players and teaching systems. **Keep It Simple** is certain to enhance your comprehension and appreciation of tennis. Also, it will probably help you win some of those close matches you otherwise might lose.

by
Steve Wilkinson, Editor
July, 1987

# CHAPTER ONE
# KEEP IT SIMPLE

## KEEP IT SIMPLE

There is an old adage, "A little learning is a dangerous thing." Having been over the road of learning sports skills from untrained, superficial observation to detailed graduate study of mechanical skills, I would add a second adage. "A great deal of learning can lead to total confusion and misdirection."

For example, just standing on the court in a vertical position is a very simple act, it seems. If analyzed in detail, however, this involves muscles, skeleton and nervous system to a degree of complexity that becomes incredible. The marvel is that we don't fall flat on our faces. Now, add a running forehand passing shot, and the degree of complexity of the performance goes completely off the scale. What saves us? We have been provided with a remarkably complex central nervous system that coordinates the whole body, all governed by an extraordinary computer, the human brain.

Add to this amazing equipment the repetition, over tens of thousands of years, of the basic movements of evasion, pursuit and throwing, and we have a solid core of instinctive performance which can be tapped extensively to shorten and simplify the learning process. It is the combination of these human factors that have formed the bedrock of my philosophy for teaching tennis.

My teaching theories are based on experimentation and testing. Through this approach I have discovered three important principles: 1) teach the volley first; 2) employ instinct; 3) present one item at a time. These three concepts comprise the very core of "Keep It Simple."

Initially, I had coached in the traditional way with heavy emphasis on the details of groundstrokes, serve, and finally the volley and overhead smash. But as I watched the young people in tournament play, I observed that they frequently needed very short swings for out-of-position shots, for countering power, and for the volley. All they had for these situations were the long, full swings which were inadequate for keeping the ball in play. Applying the principles of offense and defense which I had used in football and basketball, I saw the value of the all-court game, of being defensive when the situation called for it, and also of being able to attack at every opportunity. To do this, we needed the block and punch of the volley.

In defiance of tradition, and going to the opposite extreme in one jump, I began all my lessons with **the** volley, with the player close to the net. I quickly learned that long swings are instinctive, but short swings must be taught. The full swing instinct is so strong that we had to keep coming back to the volley constantly in order to retain the feel of a block or punch. Depending on athletic ability, we worked away from the net as quickly as possible, perhaps in the first lesson. The length of the swing increased as we approached the baseline. However, the emphasis on the volley remained heavy until the block or punch became habitual. I have had no reason to change this approach to learning tennis, only to refine it. The most frequent response from beginners has been, "Coach, you make learning **so simple!** That was great. I was successfully hitting the ball over the net in my first lesson!"

The second major principle in the "Keep It Simple" philosophy of learning and playing tennis is the emphasis on the employment of **instinct**, as that force may be appropriate. In undergraduate and graduate theory courses in my Physical Education major, I was lead to believe that I must "teach everything" in presenting the mechanics of sport skills. Apparently my future students would be helpless masses of protoplasm and would do nothing right unless properly guided. Not long ago I asked one famous tennis instructor if he ever found that his students would do some things naturally. "Oh no," he responded instantly. "You must teach **everything!**" I disagree! I challenge anyone to bring me three or four persons, not too young, who have never had a tennis racket in their hands, and within an hour I can explode that traditional attitude.

Is it not strange that instinctive behavior in animals is accepted unconditionally, but totally denied in the human realm? Humans, as a species, have been throwing, running, dodging, and pursuing for thousands of years. Are we to believe that we have acquired no instinctive responses in all of that time? Most of our games are built around those very throwing, running, and dodging movements which humans have employed for so many years. Can instinct be used in the learning of tennis? Absolutely and extensively. For everything? No. Some instinctive responses are wrong or inefficient, but the potential is very high. I wonder why this very positive tool has either been ignored or rejected for so long.

Finally, the third key principle is teaching **one item at a time** in any one practice performance. In over fifty years of coaching, I have yet to see a person who can work on several new items simultaneously.

It has been traditional to believe that in learning sports skills you must be taught "everything." If you are not shown all those details you will probably do everything wrong. According to this attitude, athletes need to be meticulously molded, item by item.

As a result of close observation of players as they sometimes reacted on impulse during periods of instruction, I began to question the "Helpless Athlete" theory. For example, I would be ready to teach the swing of the forehand drive to a class. All were lined up in structured formation, ready to perform on signal the "weight on back foot—racket back—transfer weight—forward swing—follow through" sequence so commonly used in teaching this stroke. Now and then a student would be making a beautiful swing all by him/herself. I would ask, "Have you played tennis before?"
"No."
"Where did you learn that perfect swing?"
"I don't know. Was I doing something wrong?"
"Goodness, no! Just keep on swinging."

At first, such intrusions into a nicely planned procedure were disturbing to me. After all, I was supposed to teach these uncoordinated creatures **everything**. But what if the beginner already had a perfect swing? Here was a contradiction to what I'd been taught. Was the traditional attitude at least partially wrong? Could there be some proficient, instinctive responses?

After fifty years of teaching sports skills to people of all ages and all levels of ability, I reject the concept of human physical imperfection and helplessness. Rather, I have gradually acquired a very deep respect for the capability of this marvelous mechanism we call the human body to perform many phases of the game of tennis instinctively.

At the outset, I realize there has to be the desire to perform well. And there are certain additional factors of significance in the initial performance and rate of learning. One is innate ability or coordination. Just as people vary in degree of intellectual capacity, so they vary in their innate motor capacities from somewhat less than average to the level of physical genius. There may be some "physical morons" (persons with extremely low coordination), but I have yet to see one.

Another factor in initial performance and learning rate is the extent of previous participation in games like baseball, basketball, tennis, badminton, golf, or handball. These sports have so many basic perform-ance patterns in common that participation in one is most helpful in developing the skills which are common to all.

I acknowledge the importance of these factors. Nevertheless, my primary discovery during my decades of coaching tennis has been that the human brain and nervous system compose the greatest computer complex every devised. Modern mechanical computers are primitive by comparison. Over the millions of years during which humans managed to survive by running, dodging, throwing, catching, etc., these performance patterns have been implanted in our human "computer." It needs only to be properly programmed to secure the desired outcome.

Therefore, instead of trying to teach everything, I began to search for KEY words, KEY movements, or KEY concepts from which the desired results might follow. For example, with the serve the key concept was "overhand throw." Fewer and fewer details were presented and then only as necessary. Over a period of years I learned that in some specific skills my students might do almost everything right rather than wrong. It was obvious that the basic patterns for these movements were already implanted in our nervous and muscular systems.

For example, I discovered about forty years ago that once a player is programmed for it, the two-hand backhand is a high percentage, instinctive stroke, while the one-hand backhand is poorly executed about 95% of the time. Typically, the wrist and elbow are up, the racket head is down, and the strings slice across the ball, left to right, in an ineffective stroke. Also, in many cases, muscular strength is lacking.

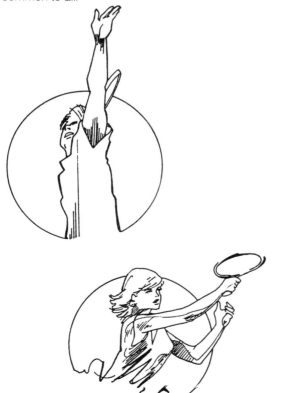

In 1948, Cynthia came to me for lessons. At 16, she was just a slip of a girl with no sports background and with no more than ordinary muscular strength. With her backhand I tried everything I could think of, with discouraging results. Finally, in desperation, I suggested we try two hands. Within five minutes Cynthia was hitting the ball with beautiful form and with control. I had a solution to the coordination and the strength problem.

But this was heresy! Why EVERYONE had always used a one-hand backhand, standard form. As I expected, traditional eyebrows were raised all over the place. Within a few years, however, two-hand backhands would virtually take over that stroke at all levels of play.

The two-hand forehand is also instinctive to a high degree. This technique also provides adequate strength often lacking with some women and children. The key concept is "swing as in softball." Often the stroke is perfect immediately, although perhaps too forceful. If the follow-through is too low, note the angle of the arms and racket at the side of the body. Maintain that angle throughout the swing. I have found that the second hand may be removed later, with no adverse effect on the stroke.

Footwork is almost 100% instinctive. Traditionally, great pains are taken to show each person how to move his or her feet. It is a waste of time. I start all beginners at the net with the volley. Assuming you are right-handed, as you make the volley I notice whether you step forward with the right or the left foot. If the step is with the left foot, we go on. If it is made with the right foot, we take a few repetitions stepping with the left foot.

Next, I warn you that the next toss may "make you run a little to reach the ball." Usually your footwork is correct immediately. On occasion you may go back to finishing with the right foot forward. If so, we do a few repetitions to finish with the left foot forward as you volley.

Recently, working with a small, nine-year-old girl, I began tossing the ball to her on the bounce more quickly than I usually do. On both forehand and backhand, her footwork was beautiful to behold. Exceptional? Not at all; rather typical. She used all sorts of combinations of skips, hops, pivots and different lengths of running steps to fit the occasion. Yes, footwork is almost 100% instinctive, thanks to thousands of years of practice by our ancestors.

What about a firm grip on the racket? If you ask me that question, I hand you a ball and tell you to throw it to the center mark on the opposite baseline. As you stand near the net, do your best to throw sharply and right on that mark. After your throw I ask if you kept a firm grip on the ball during your throw. Like everyone else, you may look a little puzzled with an expression of "Is there any other way?" That is right; is there? You instinctively hold the ball as firmly as necessary for a successful throw at the target. Take notice of my emphasis on total concentration on the target throughout your throw. Here is the MUST of quality performance in tennis, CONCENTRATION, INTENSE AND SUSTAINED.

Such concentration **must** be present if instinct is to operate to its fullest potential. If you cease to focus on the target at any point in your throw, your grip probably loosens and your total bodily coordination is lost. In tennis, we "throw" with our racket, rather than with our hand as in baseball. Since the hand controls the racket face, the grip on the handle is as firm as necessary, just as it is in throwing the ball with the hand. With total concentration, a firm grip is instinctive.

Instinct does not produce desirable form in all cases. For instance, it is definitely instinctive to use a full and frequently too powerful swing with ground-strokes. That full swing is often initially carried into the volley, where we need to "block" or "punch." The swing reflex is so strong that you may have to return again and again to practicing the short swing for the volley and for emergency shots.

Furthermore, with instinct alone, you can hardly expect a high degree of skill to emerge immediately. To attain that kind of performance, there must be many, many hours of intense drills, plus the honing of your skills to a fine edge by competitive play. Yet, after all these years of employing instinct in my teaching of tennis, I marvel at the high quality of form so frequently exhibited by beginners.

# KNOW THE KEYS TO LEARNING

If instinct is to operate efficiently in learning tennis, several sound principles of learning must be present. **First**, you must be relaxed. Anyone is likely to fear failure at first, and with that fear goes tension, a decidedly negative influence on learning. If I feel that you are tense, I will ask, "Do you worry a little? A bit tense? If so, relax. Do whatever comes naturally, even turn a somersault." I may go through a few steps of a drunken sailor routine. Silly, isn't it? But it usually gets results. You smile and relax.

**Second**, you must NEVER be asked to concentrate on more than one item in any one performance. Yes, yes, I know. It has been traditional to present many of those details of each skill on which we might be working. But, if I ask you to concentrate on even two items, you may get the first and miss the second. Or you may get the second and miss the first. Or you may become confused and miss both of them.

**Third**, the degree of difficulty of any one perform-ance must be adjusted to your present level of ability. For example, if you are a beginner, I start you with the forehand volley. You stand within three to five feet from the net. I **toss** the ball to you **underhand** from a distance of approximately fifteen feet. Overhand throw? NO! Hit the ball to you? NO! If the degree of difficulty is just a few percentage points too high, learning is seriously retarded. I increase the difficulty only as fast as your abilities permit.

A **fourth** principle of learning, the key factor in focusing the player's entire nervous and muscular mechanism, is a **target** or a specific point of aim on the court. Once the degree of difficulty is adjusted to the player's present level of ability, a target "programs" the human "computer system" and the body into a united whole. Together they focus on an effort to hit the ball close to the target. The results of this focus of effort pleasantly surprise the player. I often use my hand as a target, or a racket cover. Usually, within three to five tries, the player develops a pattern of hitting the ball close to the target. As soon as this pattern occurs, I increase the difficulty, progressing to a higher level of performance. The learning pattern is repeated with a target with every increase in difficulty.

**Fifth**, I emphasize the **positive**. Nearly all of the people who come to me for lessons grossly under-estimate their talent, so I begin to build confidence at every opportunity. No flattery, just honest praise for good performance. It does wonders for self-esteem, enjoyment **and** performance!

**Sixth**, I use **key words** or concepts to trigger instinct and help the player to visualize what is to be done. For example, with the serve the key concept is "throw overhand." For the two-hand forehand, "Swing as though you are batting in softball."

When she came to me, Jane was a sad example of violations of these principles. Her husband called to ask if I would give this 28-year-old mother some tennis lessons. Certainly, I would. He warned me that I was in for trials and tribulations because Jane had very poor coordination. The left foot didn't know what the right foot...I interrupted to say I just didn't believe it. Well, he assured me, I would see, but just do my best.

Jane came for her first lesson with two small children whom she took to the sandbox about thirty yards away. As we were about to begin, the children called for attention. Jane ran over to them; I should not say she ran—rather she "floated" over there and back. To me, Jane appeared to be a tremendous natural athlete, but she had been so indoctrinated with the low coordination tag that it took me nearly a month of two lessons a week to convince her otherwise. Her earlier instructors must have violated all six of my learning principles. Jane was a teacher's delight and her progress was phenomenal.

# DISCOVER "GROOVING"

All of your performances in tennis involve habits—physical, mental and emotional. You are always trying in practice to form good habits and refine them to a high degree of efficiency, or to replace bad habits with good ones. It is not a matter of physical habits alone, such as footwork and stroke patterns. The mental habits of sustained concentration and analysis of opponents are just as important. And the most volatile and difficult of all the habits to control are harmful emotional habits. These need to be replaced by self-confidence, courage and the quality so much sought after by coaches—DESIRE.

There is often a general lack of understanding and appreciation of the fundamentals of habit formation and change. Almost everything you do is controlled by habits. The body, mind and emotions can be trained to follow almost any pattern you desire by willful repetition. The nervous system becomes "grooved" and tends to repeat, without conscious attention, an act of any type, given the proper stimulus to set the habit pattern in motion. Much of the so-called "fast thinking" in sports is not deliberate thinking at all. It is habitual reaction to situations that have been faced many times before. Granted, you must "keep your head in the game," must concentrate on what you are doing for high-level performance, but you are still reacting in matches largely by habit.

Action is too fast for the mental processes involved in deliberate thinking. Whether a person is playing a complicated piano score during a concert, or typing from shorthand notes in the office, each involves a stimulus-response situation, a complex pattern of habits developed by endless repetitions commonly called practice. Tennis matches, too, are played on habit patterns carefully developed and refined through hours, months and years of practice and competition.

The first step in habit formation must be an **understanding** of the pattern to be followed. You, the learner, must comprehend what you are to do. You may have to think and act out each step carefully and then put the parts together slowly. There are likely many errors at first. Gradually the pieces of the total performance fall into place, however, and with a sufficient number of repetitions a smooth performance results. Thereafter, you need only the proper stimulus to set the habit pattern in motion, and with little conscious attention, you achieve a uniform performance. You have then "grooved" the habit.

As a simple illustration, you have learned through practice how to move into position and stroke a forehand drive in good form. The stimulus is the approaching ball. All the details of footwork, backswing, transfer of weight, contact and follow-through are performed automatically as a result of careful, repetitious training. The body is a marvelous, flexible machine which can be trained to perform complicated tasks almost automatically by careful and willful practice. Once formed, a habit can be depended upon when needed. You can perform at high speed, almost unconsciously, a task far too involved for deliberate thinking. Having mastered that pattern of movements, you are now free to study your opponent as you play and direct the forehand shot to any part of your opponent's court, as necessary, for winning the point.

Traditionally, in the teaching of tennis, one stroke at a time is explained to beginners. They are then asked to demonstrate the stroke. This means repeating a series of new movements that must be performed consecutively. (i.e., to hit a forehand, you must turn the shoulders, take the racket back, keep the racket parallel to the ground and the wrist firm, step forward, and follow through high, among other things). This means confronting novices with three or more actions that must be performed consecutively. Even the most athletic player becomes confused. Many beginners decide they are slow learners and/or not too well coordinated.

In learning a stroke, never attempt to concentrate on more than one item at a time. Even two items widely separated in the sequence of the stroke are too much to absorb in one performance. For example, you are asked to widen your stance on service and to finish the swing farther to your left (assuming you are right-handed). Or, on the forehand drive, you are to begin your backswing sooner and follow through higher. Although the two items in each of these examples are widely separated in sequence, you cannot work on both at the same time. Even minor changes in a habitual pattern are upsetting, and the resulting uncertainties carry through the entire stroke. Once you feel comfortable with the wide stance or the early preparation, you can go to work on the follow-through.

The one-item principle can be applied to the volley. Assume you are right-handed, and you have two faults; you step with your right foot on the forehand volley, and you contact the ball too late. Correcting the footwork is the easiest, and you deal with this first. You concentrate entirely on stepping forward with your left foot. On the first attempt you may step perfectly, but volley the ball off the rim and into the bottom of the net. Your reaction is likely to be, "That was a terrible volley." Surely, you think, anybody can step with the left foot and hit a good volley simultaneously. But you **did** step correctly, and that was the only thing that counted. Where the ball may go is of no consequence whatever at this time.

With your second try, you again step perfectly. You hit the ball just a little off-center this time. On the third try, your step is again perfect and you have gained assurance. The ball is hit in the center of the racket. Although your attention has been totally on the step, your habit pattern of hitting the ball near the center of the racket reasserts itself after being upset by the new item regarding your footwork. To reinforce the learning procedure, make one more volley and then hold your pose at the end of the stroke. As you hold your pose, you see you have stepped diagonally forward perfectly. Your knees are slightly bent, and you have excellent balance. With a total of three to five consecutive good performances, go to the next item.

Now, forget your feet entirely and work only on overcoming late contact. Your attention is directed to getting the feel of meeting the ball well out in front of your body with little or no swing. While you are making these adjustments, an observer can check to see that you do not return to the incorrect right-footed step. If you return to the old habit, go back to practicing the left-footed step for one or two performances.

After you have met the three to five consecutive good performance standard, you can forget form and concentrate only on hitting the ball down the center to your practice partner. This is a test to determine whether the volley form has become habitual. The ball may go a little high, low, right, or left at first, but you are placing it closer to your target. You are stepping correctly, and you are meeting the ball well out in front of your body with a block or punch. If you revert to your old form, stop hitting for the target and return for drill on the deficiency until you have three to five consecutive good performances. For reinforcement, pose after hitting the volley to check your form.

A similar situation may arise with your serve. For example, your feet are too close together—less than the width of a racket head apart, and the toss is too low. Correct **one** item at a time. Moving the back foot even six inches farther back will make you feel as though you are doing the splits. You are shaken, insecure, fearful. This change is going to take some getting used to.

Hit half-speed serves while becoming accustomed to the wider stance. Pay no attention to the direction of the ball or whether the serve is good or not. Very likely the first serve is hit off-center. You cannot expect to adjust to the new stance and continue to serve well at the same time.

After several more swings, you become comfortable with the new stance. As always happens, the ball is hit more cleanly as confidence returns. You are now moving your body weight from back to front foot, whereas before there was little, if any, transfer. You are hitting the ball with more power and doing it easily.

Now that the new stance is comfortable, you can correct the height, location, and starting point of the toss. Focus on the toss only. Determine the height by noting the location of the center of the racket, as you hold it with your arm fully extended upward. Establish the correct starting position for the toss by placing your racket out in front of your body at waist height with your hand holding the ball in contact with the throat of the racket. Practice the toss, hitting at half speed. Your practice partner can check on the width between your feet. Your old habit pattern is likely to draw them back to the former width.

Once you acquire a fairly accurate toss, forget the toss and attempt to place the serve into one of the service courts, with a target in mind. When the focus of attention is given to accuracy and away from the toss, you will quickly have a measure of the dependability of the two new habits. If there is a reversion to either one, go back for further repetitions on that one item.

I repeat, concentrate on only one item at a time. If you are attempting to place the ball accurately with your strokes while working on other items, such as footwork or backswing, you are making severe, if not impossible, demands on yourself. Also, if the ball is hit at you too hard while you are drilling on the footwork or backswing, the difficulty of the situation will seriously retard or break down learning. The ball must come to you slowly enough to give you plenty of time to prepare for it, depending upon the level of skill at which you are working.

**Don't measure your progress by the success of your shots while you are concentrating intently on a single item.** Progress, for example, with footwork is measured by the quality of your position when the ball reaches you. Are you sidewise, feet apart, the ball the proper distance from you? Or, is the backswing consistently following the pattern you want? If both are good, you can forget both while trying to place the ball accurately. See if the good habits persist when your attention is directed toward accuracy alone. Once you are sure that the new habits are persisting, then gradually increase the difficulty of the game you are playing.

Some players are very flexible about making changes, while others are almost totally inflexible. In any case, the one-item plan simplifies the learning process and diminishes frustration. It is far easier to learn one item at a time than to incorporate two, three or even four new movements into one smooth stroke.

To summarize the factors involved in the "grooving" of proper habits:

1. You must **want** to learn.
2. You must understand what is to be done.
3. You must sustain your concentration on the practice pattern.
4. The degree of difficulty must be adjusted to your level of performance.
5. You must not be required to think of more than one item at a time in any one practice performance.
6. You must have **patience**. Learning is **hard work**.

# PICK A TARGET

The use of a target as a tool is so important that I would like to explore its uses at greater length. A beautiful stroke by itself is of little value unless you can use it to direct the ball to a specific area of the court. A pretty stroke hit shallow is ideal for your opponent. That same drive, if hit deep or wide to the corners, can be severely forcing, resulting in opponent errors or weak returns. In short, if you are to force your opponent, **you must form habits of hitting the ball to certain target areas** on the court.

In attempting to place the ball to a target, your entire muscular, neural and mental mechanisms come to a coordinated focus under the direction of your own human "computer." You can "program" your computer to hit the ball to any specific target. For example, begin by placing an actual target, such as a racket cover, about five feet inside each way from the opponent's backhand corner. Your concentration must be intense and sustained **beyond** contact of ball and racket. I cannot over-emphasize the importance of this intensity of concentration, from the moment the ball approaches you until it hits near the target. Anything less than this gets ineffective results. But then, if you do not have concentration, intense and sustained, you can forget everything else. There is no consistent, high level performance without it.

If the ball strikes a little short, or long or wide, try to make the proper correction with the next stroke. DO NOT try to make changes in the form of your stroke. Placing the ball near the target is a matter of **feel** and not some mechanical trick. If stroke form weaknesses appear, take time out for specific form practice, then go back to aiming for the target. NEVER attempt to do two or more things in any one performance.

A target can be employed effectively with instinct to simplify the learning process. For example, Joan was taking her first lesson on the volley. Her form was sound. I told her that I would toss the ball to her right and at about waist height. "Just do your best to hit the ball back to my hands." Unintentionally, my toss was very low and about one step to her right. She went down until her right knee almost touched the floor, racket parallel to the floor and hit the ball right to the target, my outstretched hands. Her form was absolutely perfect for the low volley!

A high school boy came to me for help with his forehand drive. It had an exaggerated slice, he told me. I observed that this was indeed true. I asked him to forget his stroke for a few minutes and to concentrate exclusively on hitting the ball deep to a target area I marked, giving no attention to an occasional long drive. Just continue hitting for depth, near the target. Within a dozen or so strokes, he had unconsciously changed from the excessive slice to a very flat drive, exactly what he wanted. His "computer" had selected the most efficient way to achieve his goal.

The player in this illustration is demonstrating the effect of total concentration. With a target in mind, her form is excellent and the intensity of her focus on the ball is obvious.

Another time a young man came asking for help with his serve, saying it was going long. I asked him to demonstrate. The serve was indeed long, hitting at the base of the backstop. The swing was basically sound, but I could see that he was thinking "stroke" rather than "target," and his toss was too far back. I placed a racket cover on the center of the service line and told him to forget everything except a concentrated effort to hit that cover. His first serve went five feet beyond the baseline, the next one near the baseline, the third one in the middle of the back court, the fourth, fifth and sixth all made a nice pattern around the cover. He did not know that he had changed his toss from too far back to its correct position for his serve. I explained what had happened. He had been attempting to do two things at the same time, a no-no-no in learning tennis. His service form was excellent. Now he must concentrate entirely either on the location of his toss, **or** better yet, completely on the target. In his case, concentrating on the target proved to be effective.

Little Jon, age eleven, was a tremendous natural athlete. He had taken lessons from age seven, had countless hours of practice, and quite a little tournament play. His strokes were excellent, but choice of targets and intensity of concentration were often lacking. I watched for a minute as he practiced his serve, spraying the ball indifferently around the service court. I went over to him and asked, "Jon, will you do something for me? For the next three serves will you take any one of the three serving targets in order and do your best to hit each one?" (The targets were the inside corner, the outside corner, or straight at the opponent.) He nodded. The little rascal hit three consecutive serves within two-foot squares of each target. Wow! "Jon, do you understand what you can do with total concentration on a target?" He smiled and nodded. After about five minutes, I looked back to see Jon once more spraying his serves all over the place. It is usually not too difficult to fix mechanical habits. It is those volatile mental and emotional habits that put limits on so many players.

Many players do not handle abstractions well. For instance, if I say "Drive the ball deep to the forehand corner, five feet in each way," the results may be fuzzy at best. But if I place a target on the court, you may zero in on that target almost instantly. Beginning players are helped immeasurably by the use of tangible targets which focus their aim. Gradually, these targets become mental images in the player's mind, and racket cover targets are no longer needed. It is the concept of a target that remains one of the most important elements in performing with efficiency.

# CHAPTER TWO
# FOLLOW THE VOLLEY METHOD

I became Head Tennis Coach at the University of Iowa in May, 1947. We had a mammoth Field House in which I could set up temporary tennis courts on four different surfaces the year round. This made a fantastic laboratory for developing youngsters from eight years of age on through the varsity. Initially, I followed the traditional approach of first teaching the full swings of baseline groundstrokes, "with supplemental strokes according to plan."

As we went through that first summer of tournament play, I became convinced that my players should master the all-court game, which called for effective use of the volley. Simple? Not quite. The youngsters had a terrible time learning to use the block or punch of the volley, so much trouble that I recklessly threw away "the book," and in 1948 I took all my beginners to the net to learn the volley first. I quickly discovered that long swings are instinctive, but short swings **must be learned**. Thus THE VOLLEY METHOD OF TEACHING TENNIS came into being. I have had no reason to change this approach, only to refine it.

In tennis a full range of strokes is needed, from the full swing to the volley. The full swing is a useful implement, if you are able to prepare fully for it, and if you need that much power. But you are also going to need a block for the volley, a short swing for the half volley, a block or chip for return of power serves, fractional swings for fast activity in midcourt, and other fractional swings when you are out of position through your own misjudgment or because you are forced by your opponent. In short, you need everything from a block to a full swing, regardless of your ability level.

Contrary to popular belief, the volley is the simplest stroke in tennis. Standing close to the net, you merely place your racket in the path of the ball to block it. What is difficult is resisting the urge to swing. Your instinctive response to any approaching ball, after the bounce or on the fly, is a full swing. If you are asked to hit the ball a distance of ten feet or the entire length of the court, the response is often the same, a full swing. **Since the volley is easy and the full swing is instinctive, the solution is to introduce the volley first. This realization is the starting point for my Volley Method of teaching tennis.**

The **Volley Method** includes several important principles of learning. 1) You must be relaxed. 2) You must focus on only **one** item at a time. 3) The degree of difficulty must be presented at your level of ability. 4) Concentration must be intense and sustained. (Hits off the frame are due almost 100% to failure to watch the ball long enough.) 5) You must use a target to ocus concentration and bodily response. 6) You progress just as rapidly as your talents permit.

Using these principles, you follow a number of important steps. If you are a beginner, you start The Volley Method bouncing the ball downward on the court with your racket. This exercise gives you the feel of the ball on the strings. Then, bounce the ball upward off the racket. Take about five minutes on these exercises.

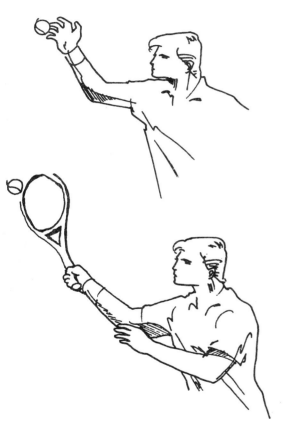

The second step in The Volley Method is to stand two to five feet (no more) from the net. Note what grip you are using. Usually, you take either an Eastern or modified Eastern forehand grip instinctively. If I am the teacher I will tell you that you are an "old smarty" by assuming the proper grip all by yourself. Positive reinforcement builds confidence, a prime ingredient in learning to play tennis.

Upon taking a position approximately fifteen feet from the net in the opposite court, I toss a ball to you **underhand** so that it reaches you at about head

height on your forehand side. You may instinctively swing at the ball, but that is a no-no with the volley. Use either a block or a punch. Visualize what happens when you hit the ball against a wall or backstop. The wall does a perfect block volley. It just stands there and it never misses. A similar concept can be gained from **catching** the ball with one hand. We toss the ball back and forth to each other, noticing that we simply **reach out** to meet the ball to catch it. There is no superfluous motion.

Next, I have you toss the ball to me, and I substitute my racket for my hand to "catch" the ball with my racket. The ball bounces back over the net to your side. Next you will "catch" the ball by using a block, or punch—a volley shot. Your errors are likely to be more a swing than a punch, or you may contact the ball late. Generally, these errors can be corrected with a dozen or so hits. As soon as you show me correct form, I may have you pose after the volley to show you that you have contacted the ball well out in front of the body and you have used no more than a slight punch. Nice going! This is to reinforce confidence and to emphasize knowledge of correct form.

Next, take a step as you make the volley. If you are right-handed and you make the step forward with your right foot, I may ask which foot you would step with in throwing the ball. Perhaps you might demonstrate such a throw. Or, after a moment's thought you may say, "My left foot." (Or right foot, if left-handed.) This, then, is what we concentrate on for a moment—your stepping forward on your left foot to make the volley. In the process, you may make some atrocious volleys, but our focus now is on stepping forward correctly. Where the ball may go has absolutely no significance. Did you make the proper step with your left foot? Yes, you did, so your performance was perfect. Let's repeat it another time or two. After four to five good practice steps, I say, "Great! We're on our way!" Then you progress to a more difficult task or a new activity.

**A target for your volleys** is our next step in The Volley Method. I suggest that you forget your form completely and just do your best to direct the ball to my hands, which I will hold out in front of me after making the toss of the ball to you. With your total concentration on hitting the target, I discover whether the new habits persist, and in addition, I introduce to you a "learning pattern" which you can employ throughout your learning experiences.

Your first attempt to hit my hands may result in a low, knee-level volley. Your form was perfect. Good!

You hit the ball directly to me, but low. See if you can come closer to the target with your next shot.

At this point I must insert an explanation of **the function and use of the target**. It tends to FOCUS your entire nervous system and your physical reactions into a coordinated whole. I have seen unbelievable responses by players using a target. You may miss the target by a considerable distance at first, but within six to eight practice shots you can be making a nice pattern of hits close to the target. You are demonstrating what I term a "learning pattern."

With continued effort and total concentration you acquire the "feel" of hitting the ball to your target. Notice that I make no suggestions as to racket angle, grip on racket, bend of knees, etc. The **feel** of the shot is what is important.

The next step in The Volley Method is to give you volleys at waist height and below, both much more difficult than the head-high stroke. With the increase in difficulty you may revert to swinging, or take the ball too late or too close to your body. If not, we go on. Corrections will usually take no more than three repetitions of the proper form.

After you have adjusted to the lower volleys, I may warn, "I'm going to make you run a little for the next volleys. Just go after them and try to hit the ball back to me." With this increase in difficulty I check your form and footwork. The tendency to swing may reassert itself, you may take the ball late, or you might finish on your right foot as you make the stroke. Frequently, your form remains perfect, and within four to six attempts you are volleying the ball right to me. Once more, as you make a volley, I may ask you to "Hold your pose at the end of the stroke so I can take your picture for **World Tennis**. The footwork was perfect. The ball was contacted well in front of the body, and you used the right amount of punch to put the ball to your target. That's great!"

Now we move to the backhand volley, nearly always using two hands. The learning pattern is almost identical to that followed with your forehand, except that I present the waist-high volley first, the low volley second, and the head high shot as the last and most difficult on the backhand. Your step is made with the right foot if you are right-handed. With the two-hand backhand you may have a tendency to drop the racket head as you make the stroke. Your racket head should point to "10 o'clock" (and "2 o'clock" on the forehand volley). Do some dry swings, then with the ball, then repeat the volley until you get the feel of the racket head remaining at "10 o'clock."

Next, take a position ten feet back from the net as I toss the ball to you from my same position, Rehearse the volley at this new degree of difficulty, forehand and backhand, with and without movement, to see if your new habits stand this test. I will use my hands as a target throughout, unless we have to make corrections of form.

At this point I introduce the "ready position"—knees bent, racket out in front of your body, feet comfortably apart. I give you several volleys to the right and then several to the left, followed by a mixture, all with plenty of time to make the necessary adjustments.

The next position you take on the court is at the service line, another increase in difficulty. Once more we check on the fundamentals of form of the volley, with and without movement, forehand and backhand. If all is well, we go to a **shortswing groundstroke** from the service line. Keep your swing short, very little more than you use for the volley.

At this point you may use much more swing than you need, since the "swing" instinct is so strong. This is a constant battle until the block or punch of the volley becomes habitual **anywhere** on the court. You could, indeed, use a much longer swing with the slow speed of my tossed ball, but in match play the ball is coming many times faster, and in this portion of the court we generally use no more than half-swings for control. I have you toss a ball at slow speed to me with you watching my swing. How long was it? Not very, because a half-swing is all we need in this situation. Always strive for simplicity. The nicest thing anyone can ever say about your game is, "You make tennis look SO SIMPLE!" That is the ultimate compliment.

Usually we reach this point in the first one hour lesson. Notice that the emphasis with form is, reach out to meet the ball with a block or punch. Concentrate on one item at a time. Why do we hit balls off-center? One reason: failure to watch the ball long enough. Hitting balls on the rim may be excusable if you are concentrating on another item, but not after that item has been learned. Footwork seldom needs attention beyond the initial steps to right or left with the volley. It is so strongly instinctive that we need only intense concentration on our game to have it work impeccably.

Next, we review volleys at the net, ten feet away from the service line, and then go to the short-swing groundstroke.

From the "ready position" I introduce **anticipation**. If I am going to toss to your right, I **look** that way and turn my body to toss that way. This is your cue to begin getting into position for the forehand **before** I release the ball. You simply turn your "ready position" to the side, backhand or forehand, as soon as possible. All movements are as simple as you can make them...and as early as possible. The two foundations on which a fine game of tennis are built are: concentration and position. No one demonstrates these two basics of concentration and early preparation better or more beautifully than Chris Evert.

Now we mix groundstrokes and volleys in random fashion. You are likely to return to a swing with the volley, instinct is so strong. But with time, the newly learned habits of block and punch stand up to playing conditions.

Next, we begin rallying from just back of the service line, with short swings. Take the volley whenever possible. If I hit some shots short, come forward, return the ball to me and then come on up to the net for several volleys. This is to emphasize the volley and to lay the basis for a later approach to the net. When you come to the net I keep my returns to you rather soft, so that you can volley with confidence. If you are playing with someone else, and that person hits the ball hard at you when you start to go up to the net, DON'T GO. Your reactions won't be quick enough, and you could get hurt and frightened. Tell your opponent to go easy to help you learn to volley confidently.

From this position, we move back toward the baseline as fast as your progress permits. Begin every lesson or practice period with volleys. Go to the net at every opportunity to refine your volleying abilities.

As one young lad, a member of my summer class remarked at the end of the session, "At the start I was scared to death at the net. Now I feel so BIG up here."

# CHAPTER THREE
# IMPROVE CONCENTRATION

## SEE THE BALL

Much has been said and is being written about strokes, grips, and footwork. But if we had perfect strokes, grips and footwork, and the most expensive racket, and a fine body, we still could not play in the dark. So, the most important fundamental of all, without which NOTHIN' works, is **seeing the ball**—which takes the necessary concentration of watching it come as close to the strings as possible.

You are tired of that old chant, of hearing the pro yell, "Watch the ball! Concentrate!" Yes, I know it is repetitive and aggravating, almost as frustrating and maddening as when we make those frame shots, most of which go into the net and mean lost points. Aren't some of those miss-hits due to bad grip, bad swing, poor footwork, wrong racket, etc.? Nope! 99.999% of those clunkers are the result of just one thing—failure to watch the ball long enough. The whole game is built on **concentration**, intense and sustained!

Can you keep your mind intently on your game throughout a match? Unquestionably this is asking too much for even an expert. The best of them lapse at times. Well, how about sustained concentration throughout a set? That would be rather tough, wouldn't it? Then, could you last through a game? Maybe through a point? You think you could? Are you sure? Well, anyway, you are **certain** you can sustain concentration through **one** stroke, aren't you? Of course! Why, anyone could...

Try this. Stand behind the baseline in serving position. **Throw** a ball like a baseball pitcher at the forehand corner of your opponent's service court. Try your best. Imagine you are a famous pitcher, whipping the third strike past a batter. Go all out! Have someone else try it, too, and watch carefully.

Notice the intense concentration by the thrower that is clearly in evidence from the moment the throw is begun until the ball has hit or missed the point of aim. See a complete transfer of weight and beautiful follow-through, with no conscious effort to attain either.

Next, stroke a ball toward the same target with your racket, using either a forehand drive or a flat or spin serve. If you make the stroke look as though you intend to **throw the racket** after the ball, if you watch the ball until it is contacted by the racket, and then if you are still looking at the target until the ball hits or misses, just as you did when you threw it, you're doing fine! **You are really concentrating**. Can you keep it up, **stroke after stroke**? If you can, you have potential as a tennis player.

But, shall we make a little wager? I'll bet somewhere in your swing you are **turning off your concentration** and letting your racket, arm and body go through the action unattended. As a result, the ball may not be coming close to your target. Even if you are concentrating throughout your stroke, I'll bet your mind is not remaining focused on the ball as it comes off your opponent's racket. Many players react to the flight of the ball only when it reaches the vicinity of the net, too late for good tennis.

Even better, are you responding to the ball **before** your opponent hits it? This is not always possible, of course, but players sometimes telegraph their intentions by body and foot position or by habitual reaction under certain conditions. For instance, you hit a forehand drive cross-court from the right corner and recover toward the center of the baseline. Your opponent may try to hit behind you most of the time, or may habitually hit down the line to your backhand. If you can detect such a tendency, you may be able to counter successfully. Although refined **anticipation** such as this may be possible only occasionally, attempting to do it sharpens your reactions to your opponent's habit patterns. At the very least, you save precious time by watching the flight of the ball **right off** your opponent's racket.

You think you **do** concentrate? Try a succession of strokes and check on it. Are you watching the ball to your own racket, and attempting to hit to a definite target on each stroke, really concentrating all the way through the stroke as you did when you threw the ball at a target? Does your attention then shift immediately to your opponent to note the direction of the return as the ball leaves the racket? Chances are you will find your mind to be a blank within one or two strokes. Or, if you last for one rally, you are apt to "blow" the next, unless you have really worked on sustaining your concentration through rally after rally.

How do we attain a high level of concentration? By just saying: "Well, let's concentrate?" Oh no! It requires the same regular practice as strokes, footwork or any other phase of the game. And, like those skills, it improves only slowly. Your head may swim at first, you may develop a mild headache or two, but such practice pays off in more accurate strokes, keener anticipation and a steadier game. With an improvement in concentration, you can win matches you have been losing.

Try counting the number of strokes per player per rally. It will seldom exceed two strokes per player. The underlying cause is often simply **a lack of sustained concentration**. I've seen many a player literally "blow-up" at having to hit and hit and hit and wait for an opening against a steady player. They usually cannot stand the mental strain, the psychological pressure of sustained rallies. We are creatures of habit, and we become uncomfortable if forced out of the grooves of our daily practice patterns.

Therefore, make the development of sustained concentration a part of your **daily practice**. It won't come in a day, a week or a month. A certain amount of progress may come quickly, but you will likely have to work hard after that to see a little progress, week by week. Perhaps you have developed habits of concentration in your study, your music, or your daily work. If so, your level of concentration in tennis will likely go upward by leaps and bounds. If you haven't done this, and if you are one of those impatient and impetuous persons, you are in for more of a struggle. Patience!

At the start of practice, give your concentration a few minutes to warm up. Like your muscles and your timing, it may be "cold." Hit at half speed. Tell yourself, "Get in position! Watch the ball!" and repeat these admonitions until you are in rhythm. Dr. Steve Wilkinson, tennis coach at Gustavus Adolphus College, has his players begin with groundstroke rallies at the **service** lines, hitting the ball **gently** to each other. They watch the ball for the kind of spin it carries and even read the trademark. This "eyeballing" right up to the strings precedes all other drills.

## THINK "ANYWHERE"

The most effective trigger for your concentration is this. NEVER assume that the ball will be hit TO you in practice or a game. Rather, assume that it may be hit **anywhere** and that you will have to GO TO THE BALL. We want perfect position just as often as it is humanly possible to attain it. NO SECOND BOUNCES in practice, either, unless the ball is completely out of reach.

Practice rallies should not end when the ball may be hit out of bounds, not if it can be reached. We are striving for SUSTAINED concentration. Keep the ball in play as long as possible. Anyway, a ball that lands out of bounds is just as good for practice as one which strikes inside the court, so why pass up an opportunity to stroke it?

Imagine this stance of a player, who is not concentrating intently at the moment the ball is to be put into play. Note that the weight is on the heels, knees straight, and the racket is close to the body. I asked such a player, Janet, if she was expecting the ball to be hit directly to her. She thinks a minute and then replies a bit sheepishly, "Yes, I guess I was." "Now," I suggest, "Assume that Mike will NOT hit the ball TO you. Rather, assume that he may hit it anywhere on the court." "Oh!" she exclaims, and unconsciously takes a different stance. A slight crouch, feet apart, racket out in front "at the ready" position. She is watching Mike's every move, ready to go to the ball no matter where it may land. This position of alertness has not been described to her. She has assumed it naturally, an instinctive reaction to my "triggering" comments.

Does this trigger immediately transform a player's concentration from wandering to sustained? Hardly! Old habits are not overcome easily. At the beginning of EVERY rally remind yourself that you may have to go ANYWHERE to respond to the ball coming over the net.

So, the next time you go out to practice, try reminding yourself at the beginning of EVERY rally, "I have no idea where the ball may go. Watch it!" I'm sure you will see a vast difference in your ability to get to the ball and in excellent stroking position if you trigger your own concentration in this way.

## USE VASSS

James Van Alen substituted the scoring system of table tennis for traditional tennis scoring. Under the Van Alen Serving and Scoring System (VASSS), one player serves five points, the opponent serves five, and so on until one player wins 21 or 31 points, with a two-point lead. The winner of the best two of three games wins the match.

From observation of player behavior in both practice and challenge matches with varsity and freshmen squad members, I believe that it has a real value in the development of sustained concentration. It seems to force the participants to go all-out on every point throughout the match. Why should this be so? Here are my guesses.

First, VASSS puts a premium on the winning of **all** points. Under traditional scoring, **certain** points have been emphasized as being **key** points, due to the nature of that scoring system. With the VASSS system, **every** point is really a key point. Every point you win is, in effect, one fewer for your opponent's score and one more toward the total of 21 or 31 that you are striving to reach to win the game. The psychological effect seems to be rather magical. Players scramble desperately in every rally!

The second reason is very similar to the first. Under traditional scoring, the emphasis is on holding your service. **Games** take primary importance because points won or lost disappear completely at the end of each game. But with the VASSS system every point that you win, on your service or during your opponent's service, stays in your credit column until a game is finished. Woe unto the player who loafs during his opponent's serve!

Third, a five-point lead can disappear so quickly that one does not dare let down for long. The first complaint of players introduced to this system of scoring is, "Gee, it really keeps the pressure on you!" Will it adversely affect your play under traditional scoring? Definitely not! No players will ever be any better than their degree of concentration. I believe that VASSS is valuable for raising any players ability to sustain concentration from the first service through match point.

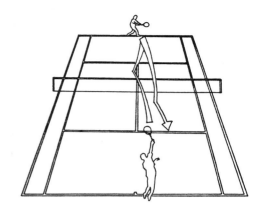

# GENERATE "CYCLES"

Concentration is the most important habit to be developed and strengthened during practice. No idle conversation! You need every bit of mental effort that you can muster. Concentration actually requires more effort than physical movement. There is a "concentration cycle" that must be endlessly repeated if your game is to have any consistency.

In detail, here are the mental processes involved in one exchange of shots, the ball being hit to your opponent and back to you. Beginning the exchange with a serve, you place your feet carefully at a convenient location back of the baseline and look the situation over. What kind of serve will you use and where will you try to place it—forehand, backhand or straight at your opponent? Fixing your target in mind, you aim for it throughout your swing and to the end of the follow-through. Your eyes then follow the ball toward its target. As the ball reaches your opponent's court, you make a mental note on its accuracy. You may need to make a correction on your next serve.

Your eyes next follow the ball on to your opponent's racket. Another mental note is made of the effect of your serve. It is handled well or is taken rather off balance. Immediately thereafter, you are attempting to determine at the earliest possible moment where the return will come in your court. Sometimes you can tell before the ball is hit, but at the worst you should know where it will come by the time it has reached the opponent's service line. Better yet, catch the direction of the ball **as it leaves the racket!** Most players fail to react before the ball reaches the net.

As you move to intercept your opponent's return, you must decide whether you will be ready for a forcing shot, be content with a neutral return, or be defensive and merely attempt to get the ball back and as deep as you can. It is silly to try to play offensively on every shot you make. Too many errors are bound to result. If you think you can play a forcing shot, select your target just as you did with your serve and aim for it **throughout your swing.**

Be careful that you do not drop your concentration for neutral or defensive shots. They must be played as carefully as the forcing shot, or you will quickly be in trouble from errors or very weak returns from which your opponent will force you strongly.

This completes a "concentration cycle." It will be repeated over and over. Actually, much of the detail involved can become automatic. However, concentration, like strokes, must be drilled on daily if it is to become an asset. Many players, accustomed to short rallies and consequent short periods of concentration blow sky high as their concentration endurance is exhausted by sustained hitting. We may run players until they are physically exhausted. Isn't it just as smart to exhaust their concentration endurance? Developing sustained concentration is difficult but most profitable in building a winning game!

# CHAPTER FOUR
# DEVELOP STRATEGY

## UNDERSTAND PERCENTAGES

Percentage play is widely applied and respected in all sports. It is a **must** for consistent winning when competitors are evenly matched. Bill Tilden once remarked that matches are never **won** (by placements) but are actually **lost** (by errors). Seldom does a winner make more than 35% placements against 65% errors. That is, for every 35 points won by placements you **give** away 65 points through your own errors. More commonly the percentages are 20% placements and 80% errors. To put it another way, out of every 100 points that you win, 20 of them come from your own placements and the other 80 from your opponent's errors.

If you think over these figures objectively, it is obvious that the average player is willing to **give away** four points on errors in order to gain one point by a placement. There may be more emotional pleasure in making a placement, but are you playing for this or to win?

Am I implying that "All I do is just hit the ball back?" Far from it! Simply take a little more care to keep the ball in the court and be willing to accept opponent errors for just what they are, each a point toward winning your match and each just as valuable in that respect as are placements. Let your opponent gamble with the four to one odds. Cut your errors to a three to two ratio, and you can win easily. Tennis should be played with the deepest respect for these percentages. Unfortunately, too many tennis players equate steady tennis with dinking and pushing. Steadiness does not **have** to be merely "push ' n pray." It is not an absolute term at one end of the scale with its absolute opposite, the "hitter," at the other end of the scale. Smart players can adjust their emphasis according to their own games on any one day and according to their opponents on the same day. Steadiness is a quality of **consistency** which permits you to win **just a little over half the points**. By being just a little steadier and reducing your error percentage, you may be able to pick up enough extra points to win the close matches.

## START EARLY

Traditionally, the introduction of strategy is delayed until all strokes are "soundly established," whenever that is. I believe in developing strategy coincidentally with the learning of strokes for beginners of all ages. Can I expect beginners to apply strategy? Absolutely, and have a lot of fun doing it! We begin with very simple strategy and develop it to greater complexity as their games become more varied.

Using the volley method, we are soon rallying between the service lines. You are stroking in good form and can sustain a rally for several strokes. I ask you, "Are you by nature just a little mean, a bit nasty?" Silly question, but you will get the point and grin in anticipation. I tell you, "Now all friendship ceases. I want you to run me all over the court. Where can you hit the ball to give me trouble?"

"Toward the line on your forehand."

"Right. Where else?"

"Toward the line on your backhand."

"Right again. Where else?"

That stumps you so I point to my feet. You are surprised. "What? Hit a ball right **to** you?" "Oh, yes, one of the best shots in the game."

We begin the rally and you hit to my right. I go over, make the return and stay to the side to emphasize the wide open court to my left. You make a fine passing shot. (Strategy principle: Open up the court with **one** shot, then pass or force with the next.)

In the next rally you run me to the left. I make the return and stay to the left, but you hit the ball right back to me. "S-a-a-y! I thought you were mean. What a sweet opponent I have. Where should the ball have

been placed?" With a sheepish reply, "To your right." We repeat the situation until you make three consecutive passing shots to my right. Immediate repetition in the correction of errors can increase the rate of learning by 10-20 times. (Strategy principle: hit the ball to the obvious open court. Make it simple.)

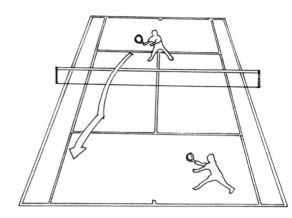

In the next rally you hit the ball into the net or perhaps too near the sideline. We stop for analysis. Where should the ball strike the court? Answer, at about the service line and four feet within the court. (Strategy principle: never hit the ball any harder or any closer to the lines than is necessary to win the point.)

You are making too many errors on the third or fourth shot, mostly due to poor concentration resulting in rim shots. Many opponents have this same weakness, inability to sustain concentration. We begin a little game of rallying between the service lines in which I make no errors and you must make at least four good strokes to win a point. You lose the first game 10-5. What happened? You GAVE me the game by your own errors. (Strategy principle: tennis matches are usually LOST by errors, not WON by placements.)

Next we work on a simplified three-stroke sequence of attack from just back of the service line. I toss the ball to you. You drive the ball to any one of our three established targets. My next toss places the ball about half way to the net. You come forward, drive for one of the targets and immediately come forward to the net for an easy volley, again, to one of the targets. This is the basic plan of attack whether from groundstroking or following the serve to the net. We repeat this pattern several times until you are familiar with the sequence. Then we resume rallying in which

I set up the sequence over and over again. (Strategy principle: approach the net with a three stroke sequence in mind.)

We move back to the baseline and I "play-act" a typical opponent. After a few minutes you tell me which is stronger, my forehand or my backhand. My forehand, right? To which side will you place your shot? To my backhand. We continue to rally and I notice that you do the natural thing of hitting most of your shots to my forehand, crosscourt, so I give you some trouble with my strong forehand. I stop the rallies to ask if you are aware that you are hitting more than half of your shots to my forehand? Play my backhand. You try, but find that you unconsciously come back to my forehand. (Strategy principle: know where you are hitting the ball. Keep the opponent's weakness in mind and place the ball accordingly.)

Next, I play the part of the heavy hitter who is not very steady. (Strategy principle: counter power with steady, soft drives well above the net.)

Next, I play the very steady player who makes very few errors. (Strategy principle: rally until you get a short ball, and then attack.) Now I become the baseliner who never comes to the net unless forced to do so. I pass and lob well. (Strategy principle: draw the opponent to the net and then pass or lob.)

Next, I draw you to the net and pass you with a wild swing, the ball hitting the line. Let's evaluate my shot. Was it a well-controlled shot? No! How often could I make it? Maybe one in twenty, so don't worry about it. (Strategy principle: don't worry about occasional, lucky shots.) But, if I play the shot with a smooth swing under control, it may be one of my pet shots, which we all have. Say it was a crosscourt passing shot. Your approach shot was good. A little later I pass you again. Yes, it appears to be a stroke in which I have confidence, so next time you play over a step to cover it. (Strategy principle: take away your opponent's strength by an adjustment of your position.) Will I recognize your move and counter it by going down the line? Maybe or maybe not. (Strategy principle: NEVER assume that your opponents will do ANYTHING until they prove they CAN AND WILL.)

We now begin rallies in which you are to observe the effects of depth on my strokes, an extremely important item in competitive tennis. I help you by calling "deep" when your drives come within five feet of the baseline. I will play-act the three common outcomes of depth on your opponent. One is netted errors. The second outcome is often a weak, short

return which strikes the court within the service courts, maybe just over the net. And third, a high, slow floater, purely defensive. With such a scenario you will have many opportunities to attack IF you learn to watch the ball to its contact with my court. (Strategy principle: recognize the value of keeping the ball deep.)

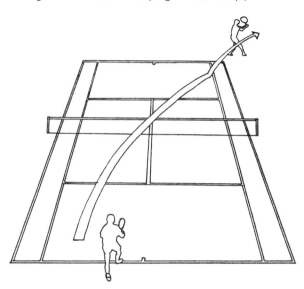

In summary, **never go into a match thinking strokes**. Stroke production is refined to dependable habits in practice. In a match you want your mind free to observe your opponent and to apply your abilities effectively to win that match. Furthermore, a critical item in average play is steadiness.

Probably the most important single item in average play is **steadiness**. But how we love to "hit the ball"— and make too many errors in doing so! Tennis is, or **ought to be**, a game in which **intelligence and percentage play** dominate the strategy. Your opponent can be played on physical, mental and emotional bases, not just on the mechanical factors. This makes the game as broad and as deep as human nature itself. The utterly ridiculous emphasis on "hitting the ball," a synonym for silly over-hitting, is an insult to human intelligence. You can learn to enjoy tennis as a game of matching wits as well as muscle.

## EMPHASIZE DEFENSE

So much emphasis has been placed on offense in tennis that defense is badly neglected or even ridiculed. Derogatory terms like "dinker" and "pusher" discourage some players from doing anything other than "hitting" (slam-banging) the ball. They feel they must attempt to play an offensive game, the so-called "big" game, all the time. This reminds me of untrained boxers who swing wild punches with no discrimination and little defense. Occasionally one or the other is hurt by a lucky blow, but most of the match, like average tennis, consists of a series of misses—a comedy of errors.

Tennis players, like boxers, must learn when to hit offensively and when to "cover up." That is, a forcing stroke by the opponent should be parried with a defensive return. A smart tennis player can often beat a much stronger opponent with good defense **and** offensive strokes when good openings occur. A well-balanced game calls for a defense against an opponent's attacking shots, coupled with crisp, offensive strokes **when the opportunities arrive**.

In the minds of many, there seems to be no middle ground where offense and defense are concerned. You are either one extreme or the other. There is no shading in the quality of strokes from offensive to neutral and on into purely defensive returns. You are either a dinker or a hitter. How silly! All other sports **emphasize** defense. Teams take pride in being recognized for their defensive ability. Why should we neglect it so badly in tennis? Why this ridiculous emphasis on offense to the exclusion of defense?

Tennis differs strategically from most sports in its method of scoring. In football, basketball and baseball, an error will merely present the opponents with an **opportunity** to score. Once the opportunity is gained, they must still capitalize on it. In this attempt, the initiative may be lost and the scoring opportunity is gone. But in tennis, an error on your part **gives** your opponent a point instantly, with no follow-up needed. You can see why we often say that tennis matches are not won; they are **lost**! That is, lost through errors, not won by placements. As you consider how unique tennis is, in this respect, could anything indicate more clearly the importance of defense?

What do we mean by defensive tennis? As an illustration of a purely defensive yet effective game, here is a true story from one of our annual Big Ten tennis tournaments several years ago.

Bob, one of my players, had some of the most fluid and beautiful flat drives I have ever seen. He could hit a bullet-like ball with remarkably little effort. However, he tended to over-hit and hence make many errors.

In the second round of the singles, he played a courageous opponent named Steve, whose strokes were inferior, but who possessed plenty of will to win. During the course of the match, I noticed that Bob was stroking well and that Steve was scrambling all over the court, desperately returning Bob's shots as best he could. In one game, Bob hit two clean placements past Steve from the baseline. I noted also that he was making his usual high percentage of errors.

In a surprisingly short time, the boys came off the court, the match finished. Bob's uniform was clean and he was barely perspiring. Steve, by contrast, was sweaty and soiled from head to foot. He had taken numerous falls while lunging for Bob's drives into the corners.

"Score, Bob?" I inquired.

"Aw, he won 6-2,6-2," grunted Bob. "My forehand wasn't working too well." He slouched off to the fountain.

I turned to Steve, "Congratulations, Steve. You certainly showed what determination and defense can do."

"He should have won," apologized Steve. "He was really hitting the ball. I wasn't"

"Now, you know better than that, don't you, Steve?" I chided.

"Well, what else could I do? I couldn't hit with him. He was too powerful for me. All I could do was run and try to hit the ball back as best I could."

"Precisely," I agreed. "You threw up the best defense that you could muster. You got most of the shots back. He made too many errors in his attempts to be aggressive. You played it smart and won. Don't apologize for playing defensive tennis to win. The person at the scoreboard doesn't ask **how** you won, but **did** you!"

"Thanks, Coach. Thanks a lot. I hadn't really appreciated winning by means of a defensive game."

Steve played purely defensive tennis—and won, or should we say, rather, that Bob lost. The mistake so common in average tennis is the attempt to hit all strokes offensively, and most strokes are hit offensively without enough thought about ability to **keep them in the court.**

You usually find yourself in defensive situations for two reasons: 1) as a result of good shots by your opponents; 2) due to your own errors in footwork and judgment, leaving you in a poor position to stroke well. In either case, do your best to get the ball back over the net with a minimum of errors. Make the defensive return as **deep** as you can, but get it back!

The percentage of errors made in attempting to return forcing shots **offensively** is too high. It is not intelligent tennis. A defensive return would reduce this error percentage to a low figure. Furthermore, you force your opponent to make at least one more stroke in trying to win the point. Your defensive returns keep the pressure on your opponent to sustain his/her hitting. Don't apologize for defensive returns. Take pride in them. I've observed that **nearly half of all defensive returns results eventually in points for the defensive player,** because a return that you thought was going to be defensive may inadvertently be offensive because of the depth on angle. Be sure you watch the ball to its court position!

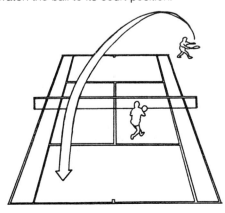

If your opponents follow their forcing shots to the net, don't hesitate to throw up lobs, particularly if you are off balance. Try to make your lobs fall into the back court. Few average players have effective overheads when forced to hit them from back of the service line. Make practice on lobs part of your daily workout.

Average players sometimes apologize for lobbing. Good players take pride in it. Let me remind you that lobs can be offensive as well as defensive. So don't regard lobs as "dink" shots to be despised, but valuable offensive and defensive strokes to be employed as a regular part of your balanced game.

Tennis is a great game. It possesses the full range of strokes from the delicate finesse of a drop shot to the solid power of the cannonball serve. There's a constant play of emotions and a complexity of psychology during every moment of a competitive match. The hard-earned skill of fine stroking must be supplemented with the intelligent application of strategy.

# BE SMART ON "OFF" DAYS

Tennis matches are generally contests in which you compete against a standard which you have set for yourself, rather than against your opponent on the opposite side of the net. Your standard for performance in match play is commonly the very maximum ability on your best days. Providing that your opponent is believed to have at least equal ability to play the game, you strive desperately to achieve this self-imposed standard. All strokes are expected to be operating at or near their best in power and accuracy. If your expectation is realized (if you are "hot"), you usually win and are quite happy with your match. In case both you and your opponent are at your respective peaks, both of you may come out of this match quite satisfied with yourselves, win or lose. However, if you are not quite up to the standard you have set for yourself, you probably become disgruntled with your strokes, yet keep banging away, hoping to get "on your game" before the match is over. Meanwhile, you are producing a generous series of errors to hasten your opponent's victory. You are simply giving the match away by means of your own errors, and seldom achieve the standard you are hoping to attain.

Now and then all players experience those days when they cannot seem to do anything wrong. It is indeed, a thrill. But what is to be done when the errors are piling up? Probably both players are equally frustrated with their games, yet neither is likely to be conscious of the other's frustration. Any relationship of their own performance to that of their opponent's is regarded as purely coincidental.

Ask yourself two simple questions. One is, "**How well can I play today?**" There is no use expecting to be at your best day after day. You won't be. Besides, if your opponent is known to be good enough to give you trouble, or to be a better player, you are very likely to set your standards of performance for yourself higher than if you expect to win by a comfortable margin. This usually means you are asking yourself to produce a game that is well beyond your present ability.

As the match begins, go ahead and attempt the quality of game you **want** to play. If you are "hot," just keep going through to match point. But if you are not "hot," do not **give** the match away with errors. The simplest solution is to reduce the number of your errors. Do not hit quite so hard or so close to the lines. Use a greater margin of safety. Of course, do not go from overhitting to the other ridiculous extreme of just "pushing" everything down the middle. Simply play a **little** safer so that the rallies last a little longer, until you have some good opportunities for forcing your opponent. Also, this gives your opponent more opportunities to make errors. At any rate, **make sure** that your opponent must really **win** at least half the points he/she gets with placements or forced errors. Do not just give away the match with your own errors.

Decide whether to keep on attempting your usual game and hope it will come back, or do the best you can with what you have today. Take a careful look at the situation. Perhaps it isn't as bad as you think. You may be able to capitalize on your strong points for the day, avoid the weaknesses, and still pull out a victory.

Are you hitting some shots very well and others not so well? Maybe your backhand is stronger than usual, but your forehand is not up to par. Then be defensive on the forehand and hit out with the backhand. Your ground strokes are not so good, but your volleys are great? Get to the net! You can't hit either of these strokes well, but you can run, bloop and lob? Then do just that, if it works. The aim is to **win**, not to put on an exhibition of strokes. The umpire gives you no credit for **form**. You can win only by means of **points**. Let's face it! Most of these will be by your opponent's errors.

There is also a second simple question which you need to ask yourself. "**How well must I play to win?**" This depends on your opponents. Before going down for the third time in your sea of despairing errors, look over their game. How are they playing today? Maybe they are not as tough as you thought. Perhaps they are having a bad day too. And to help you along your rocky way, they may not have detected that you aren't "up." Anything that can happen to you may also happen to them. You miss shots you shouldn't miss? Take note! They just missed a setup volley. They shouldn't have missed it? No, but they **did** miss it, and they give plenty of evidence of being worried as they go to the baseline. Are you watching them closely? They are definitely off their game. Here is a chance to win when you thought you were a goner.

Play it steady, force judiciously when you can, but **give** away very few points. Allow and help them give **you** points through their errors. Play as well as you can, but don't over-play or you give them points. Your placements and your opponent's errors count equally. Both help your victory, with 65% to 85% of your points coming from their errors. Furthermore, by playing steadier and making fewer errors you may gain confidence and play with more assurance. Your opponents may think you are playing well. They are not likely to discover the truth unless you divulge it after the match. **By playing within your ability today** you have avoided giving the match away through your own errors!

If, after trying this type of play you still lose matches, you at least have done the best you can. It may have been that your opponents were "hot," or they may have had too much "stuff" for you. However, you **did not give** matches away. You made your opponents **earn** their victories. You tried everything you had. You experimented with different styles of play. Thereby you have made valuable progress in learning to evaluate your game and your opponents under fire. You are learning to be sensitive to their game, their strengths and their weaknesses and balancing them off against yours. You are on your way to playing with your head as well as with your racket.

# HIT DEEP WHEN EXTENDED

You may have noticed that when you are running wide and reaching for either forehand or backhand drives, the shot generally goes into the net or strikes your opponent's court at an unfortunately shallow place. With such a long extension of your arm, the racket face is likely tilted forward just enough to make the drive go into the net. This is also true of shots attempted when you are running hard toward the net, or falling back to take an opponent's deep drive to your baseline. Unless you learn an effective compensation for these specialized situations, the errors pile up. Let me suggest two ways to compensate.

First, as you realize that you are reaching the ball, tell yourself to "HIT THROUGH—HIT THROUGH!" That is, emphasize your follow-through much more than you usually do. This technique helps keep your racket face in its normal stroking position and insures a good, solid drive.

Another way of compensating which achieves the same result is to say to yourself as you reach the ball, "Drive the ball much higher above the net than usual. HIT DEEP!" Either one of these reminders is effective, so you can take your pick.

Now we are in the business of habit formation again. The quickest way to establish the new habit is to have a friend stand at the service line and hit the wide drives to you. Perhaps a dozen or so shots of each type is sufficient to put you on your way. **Concentrated practice** like this is many times more effective than waiting for the situations to occur naturally.

# GET THE BALL BACK

Anyone can get caught by a great shot from the opponent. You may find yourself in situations varying from late preparation all the way to total desperation, with no time to get into good position for a normal, full swing. The racket face is probably out of alignment. You can expect 80-90% errors, hardly a favorable percentage for winning tennis. In this case, traditional form may need to be forgotten. Use any technique available to get the ball back over the net, taking a chance that something good will happen.

That "something good" will be a shift from 80-90% losers to approximately 58% winners for players of average level if they can make any sort of return that falls within their opponent's court. Unbelievable? It sounds wild, but I verified this percentage in two different tests using the better juniors in the Iowa area.

To make a play on out-of-position shots, you must shorten your swing dramatically. Think "volley" with a block or punch stroke, trying to contact the ball well in front of the body. Attempt to clear the net by at least five to six feet, aiming the ball in the general direction of the center of the opponent's court. Use a block, punch, chop, push, dink—anything to get that ball back over the net and keep it in play. If you can go from 80-90% losers to 58% winners by modifying your strokes for these emergencies, who cares about perfect form?

The typical reaction to "Get the ball back at all costs" is, "If I do that I'll give them a set-up and I'll get killed by the next shot." This is true, at the upper levels of play, but most players have not learned to put away a set-up with control and crisp power. They overhit or try for the lines with resulting errors. The shot is so easy that they often fail to achieve good position, or even to watch the ball, and the opportunity is blown.

Second, few average players can make two good shots in succession. In an attempt to put a quick end to the rally, they frequently overplay the next shot and errors result. Occasionally, they are so surprised by the "lucky" return that they are not ready or in position for anything that comes back over the net.

Finally, the desperate return may in fact become a difficult shot to return. It may go deep, along a sideline, or barely over the net. Few average players can hit the ball from all areas of the court. The ball may skid low or take a high bounce. Each situation calls for judicious placement of the return according to the total situation on the court. Inexperienced players may not know what to do with the ball to make an effective return. They become unsure and, as a result, over-play the shot, making an error or just a weak return. Your "just getting the ball back" pays off!

# IMPROVE THROUGH CHARTING

A simple system for charting tennis matches is necessary. Without exact and objective figures, the evaluation of play, both under practice and match conditions, can become subjective and may amount to a controversial stand-off of one person's opinion versus the judgment of another. Factual data makes the evaluation of match play objective. Charting has been extensively used in other sports with meaningful results and could be applied to tennis. With data such as this, there can be almost immediate feed-back for the player, and it clarifies, in a literally "graphic" way, where there is need for improvement.

The point is the basic item in tennis scoring. Points are derived from three sources: 1) balls hit into the net ("N"): 2) balls hit out of court, either wide or long ("O"); and 3) placements ("P"). Placements can be subdivided into clean aces and forced errors, but for play analysis they can be combined into one item—placements. I added another category, "S" for service, to indicate whether the first or second serve is successful.

A chart in its simplest form is used to record the play of Chris and Nick while they play a practice set. In the first two games the recording symbols are vertical lines to indicate errors and placements. Service is recorded by a number one (1) if the first serve is good, or by a number two (2) if the first serve is missed.

## GAME ONE, SIMPLE CHARTING

Nick serves first. His first serve is good. Chris ends the rally with a net error. Second point—Nick's second serve is good. He ends the rally with a net error. Third point—a second serve for Nick, and he ends the rally with an out error. Fourth point—Nick gets the ball in play with his first serve, and Chris makes another net error. Fifth point—second serve is good and Chris makes an out error. Sixth point—Nick's first serve is good, and he wins the point with a placement for a one-game lead in the first set.

## GAME TWO, SIMPLE CHARTING

Now Chris will serve, and the recording proceeds in the same fashion. He loses the game and Nick leads two games to none.

Suppose that these two games are more or less typical of the play of these boys throughout the set. It becomes obvious that both boys are making far too many net errors in relation to out errors, especially since both are essentially baseliners. **Net clearance by the ball in baseline driving should be no less than 1½ to 2 feet.** Both should be trying for depth; hence, they should show many more out errors than net errors.

SIMPLE CHARTING
Games 1 and 2

| NICK | Game1 | | | | | | Game2 | | | | | |
|---|---|---|---|---|---|---|---|---|---|---|---|---|
| N | | 1 | | | | | | 1 | | | | |
| O | | 1 | | | | | | | | | | |
| P | | | | 1 | | | | | | | | |
| S | 1 | 2 | 2 | 1 | 2 | 1 | | | | | | |

| CHRIS | | | | | | | | | | | | |
|---|---|---|---|---|---|---|---|---|---|---|---|---|
| N | 1 | | | 1 | | | 1 | | | | 1 | 1 |
| O | | | | 1 | | | | 1 | | | | |
| P | | | ′ | | | | | | 1 | | | |
| S | | | | | | | 2 | 1 | 2 | 1 | 2 | 2 |

Several years ago, I did an extensive study of these two factors in the scoring of points in tennis, and I found that a totally disproportionate percentage of errors were made into the net. If a player is **aiming** for depth in baseline driving, there should be very few net errors.

Looking at the chart, we find that Nick has only one placement for three errors, while Chris has one for seven. These percentages are typical of average play. High error-low placement ratios generally result from lack of concentration and the over-playing of shots; that is, hitting too hard and too close to the lines. The players try so hard to **win** points that they often succeed in **losing** to their opponents by trying for a degree of power and accuracy which is beyond their control **at this point** in the development of their game.

The chart tells us that Nick is making 50% of his first serves good, which is not too bad; 60% to 80% would be better, of course. Chris is requiring four second serves to only two first serves. Is he having mechanical trouble? Possibly, but much more likely he is the victim of the same two faults affecting his other strokes—failure to concentrate and over-hitting.

The value of such charting is that these figures are totally objective. Anyone with a simple knowledge of the game can record them. And, there can be no argument with the facts.

For the next two games, a more complete system of recording is used. "F" and "B" represent forehand and backhand drives. A little "v" with either an "F" or a "B" (Fv or Bv, for example) is a forehand or backhand volley; "hv" is a half-volley; "l" is a lob; "cc" a cross-court; "ps" a passing shot; "a" an approach shot; "rs" a return of service. "SA" is a service ace and "OH" is an overhead smash. The numbers above the symbol indicate the length of the rally in total strokes for both players.

## GAME THREE, ADVANCED CHARTING

Nick begins with a first serve put into play. Chris makes a net error with an attempted forehand passing shot on the fourth stroke (Fps-4). Nick's second serve is good, but he hits a backhand volley into the net with the third stroke (Bv-3). On the third point Nick's first serve is good and he gets a placement with an overhead smash on the fifth stroke (OH-5). In the fourth point Nick makes his second serve, but loses the point by Chris's forehand lob placement on the sixth stroke (Fl-6). Nick's first serve is good, but he hits a backhand halfvolley into the net on the third stroke (Bhv-3). With the sixth point Nick gets a service ace placement (SA). He begins play with his second serve at the 7th point, netting a volley on the 5th stroke (Fv-5). He loses the game with an overhead smash into the net (OH-7). Nick now leads, two games to one.

NICK

| N |  | 3 Bv |  |  | 3 Bhv |  | 5 Fv | 7 OH |
|---|---|---|---|---|---|---|---|---|
| O |  |  |  |  |  |  |  |  |
| P |  |  | 5 OH |  |  | SA |  |  |
| S | 1 | 2 | 1 | 2 | 1 | 1 | 2 | 2 |

CHRIS

| N | 4 Fps |  |  |  |  |  |  |  |
|---|---|---|---|---|---|---|---|---|
| O |  |  |  |  |  |  |  |  |
| P |  |  |  | 6 Fl |  |  |  |  |
| S |  |  |  |  |  |  |  |  |

## GAME FOUR: ADVANCED CHARTING

On Chris's serve he misses the first but makes the second serve good. A forehand approach shot on the fifth stroke goes into the net. After a second serve by Chris on the second point, Nick comes up with a backhand crosscourt placement with the sixth stroke. In the third point, Chris's first serve is good and Nick ends the rally with a backhand drive out on the sixth stroke. The fourth point finds Chris serving a doublefault into the net. The fifth point occurs when Nick hits a game winning overhead smash on the eighth stroke. Nick leads in the set 3-1.

Game 4

NICK

| N |  |  |  |  |  |  |  |  |  |  |
|---|---|---|---|---|---|---|---|---|---|---|
| O |  |  | 6 B |  |  |  |  |  |  |  |
| P |  | 6 Bcc |  |  | 8 OH |  |  |  |  |  |
| S |  |  |  |  |  |  |  |  |  |  |

CHRIS

| N | 5 Fa |  |  | DF |  |  |  |  |  |  |
|---|---|---|---|---|---|---|---|---|---|---|
| O |  |  |  |  |  |  |  |  |  |  |
| P |  |  |  |  |  |  |  |  |  |  |
| S | 2 | 2 | 1 |  | 2 |  |  |  |  |  |

We can determine from this record that Nick follows his serve to the net while Chris does not. All but one of Nick's errors after his service are netted volley errors, and his one placement is an overhead smash. Chris shows no volleys and is apparently drawn to the net by short returns from Nick as he nets two approach shots—one forehand and one backhand. This shows a lack of practice on a vital stroke which should be hit deep, not close to the top of the net. His other errors are a backhand drive and a double fault. Note that Nick's errors are into the net, a flaw that is much too common. Those first volleys should be aimed deep, not to strike in midcourt or closer to the net. He would be a sitting duck for Chris's next passing shot after the short volley.

Note also that the boys get into trouble very often after second serves. They give their opponents trouble much more often with first serves. A first serve is worth a great deal just as a first serve.

This more detailed charting requires practice by the recorder. Once the symbols are memorized, a couple of hints may be useful. When a player is ready to serve, place the point of the pencil in the proper box after S. If the first serve is good, indicate so immediately. If not, record a 2 at once.

To keep track of the number of strokes, count only the server's strokes, one with the serve; then 3-5-7- etc. The receiver's stroke count is the even number. Occasionally the recorder fails to keep up with the play, but a few missed points are not significant in the total record. Certainly you have a detailed, accurate and effective record of match play for analysis and as a guide for progressive improvement. The boys should play practice drills which help them overcome their weaknesses. Future charting accurately measures their progress.

# FORCE PSYCHOLOGICALLY

Power, depth, and accuracy are usually associated with a forcing game in tennis. These factors keep your opponent off balance, gain forced errors and make outright placements. This is a "mechanically" forcing game. The **psychologically** forcing game, by contrast, is more subtle. It focuses on the mental and emotional limitations of your opponents.

One such limitation is the lack of sustained concentration. Few players learn to sustain their rallies, to play as steadily as necessary to win points, either in practice or matches. This is usually due to the player's inability to sustain a close concentration on the game for more than two strokes. After that the player is merely hitting the ball in the general direction of the opponent's court, with no particular target. The result is usually a net error. Call this two-stroke rally a "habit level." That is the normal level of their mental endurance.

In making such opponents return the ball **more** than two strokes per rally, you are forcing them psychologically, just as truly as if you were forcing them mechanically by running them from side to side or putting extra sting into your serves or volleys. It is a subtle kind of forcing and often more effective than mechanical forcing. Most players can endure far more physical than mental or emotional pressure of the kind just described.

A second mental/emotional limitation is the compulsion to over-play strokes. Players try for **great** shots far too often. Their desire to hit outright winners leads them to attempt difficult placements far too often. Naturally we get a thrill out of a clean ace. But what is the cost? According to the charts, the cost is from three to five or more outright errors for every placement.

Play your game as well as you can, but do not fall into the trap of over-playing to the point at which you make more errors than your opponent. **Keep the ball in play.** Let your opponents try to win directly by making great shots. They are almost certain to make three or four errors for every placement they score against you, because that is the emotional habit they have formed. They are trying for shots which they are incapable of making more than once out of every three to five times.

Keep the ball in play without softening your game or giving them "set-ups." Try to play **well**, but **within your ability** at the moment. It is a fine distinction to make at first. Learn to become sensitive to your opponents' game and how well you must play to swing the balance in your favor. Make this a part of your **daily practice.**

Do not gamble against unfavorable odds to win by great shots yourself if you can wait for your opponents to give you points through their tendency to overplay their game. If you can force them mechanically and psychologically at judicious moments, you increase their tendencies to over-play. Each of their errors contributes **one more point** toward your victory. **Always remember that in tennis your opponents' errors count just as much toward your score as your own placements!**

Does this mean that you get no placements for yourself? Not at all! You simply are not trying for them in the face of heavy odds. As you push them beyond a two-stroke rally, their tendency to gamble, to over-play, will become intensified. The psychological pressure will mount with every shot.

A third limitation is your opponents' tendencies to hit the ball away from you, trying to put it **beyond your reach**. By your position on the court you can actually win points without even getting your racket on the ball.

For example, when volleying, even eight to ten feet from the net, you put pressure on your opponents to make a winning shot. They will often make net errors, however, as their passing shots drop lower and lower. They may take a wild swing in an attempt to blast one past you and hit the ball far over the baseline. Or they may play it so far to the side that it is out of bounds. Each error of this type is due to their desire to keep the ball **beyond your reach**, to make a clean winner.

You must not expect this or any other plan to win **every** point. What you want is a method that wins better then **half** of the time. The questions you must answer as you plan strategy for your various opponents are: how much can you force them mechanically **and** psychologically **to induce errors**? How quickly do they begin taking reckless chances? Remember, you are probably playing ordinary players with many weaknesses.

# CHAPTER FIVE
# REFINE YOUR STROKES

## CHANGE STROKES CAUTIOUSLY

Tennis magazines give extensive coverage to THE forehand drive, THE backhand drive, THE volley, and so on. There seem to be countless instructors who try to make ALL their players conform to these stereotyped models. One well-known pro is quoted as saying, "When you come to our camp expect to have your strokes completely rebuilt. We will show you how it is done RIGHT. Then you go home and practice, practice, practice!" Simple, isn't it? Or is it?

For beginners, those basic strokes about which so much is written are indeed sound. They lay an excellent foundation on which to build a winning game. But what about changing **your established strokes** to fit these standard patterns? Is there only ONE way to hit a forehand? ONE grip? ONE stance? ONE backswing? For whom? Overall, does it really matter whether the backswing is flat, elliptical, or circular? It may be very important to you which one you use, but not all other players will use this **same** backswing.

An attempted change of form can have a devastating effect on your confidence and consequently on your entire game. Opponents you formerly beat with ease may subsequently be running you right off the court. Proceed with caution in attempting stroke changes. There are no hard and fast rules. One simply has to use mature judgment. Following are three questions you should ask yourself when confronted with the decision to change or not to change your form.

**First**, how flexible are you in adjusting to changes in grip, stance, or strokes, even of a minor nature? People vary from almost total rigidity to quite a fluid adaptability at the other end of the scale. I have been able to detect no important relationship to age, sex, race, intelligence or any other factor except the length of time a performance pattern has been in use. In general, the longer it has been in use the more difficult it will be to change.

The point I want to make is that people are not machines on which we can reset the dials and thereby change performance at will. On the contrary, they are very sensitive creatures of habit—physical, mental, and emotional. This **must** be so, or practice would be useless. There is a built-in resistance to change as a necessary part of our being.

In your own development of sound mechanics in tennis, it is important to establish the basics so firmly in your nervous and muscular system that they can stand up to the most severe demands of match play without any conscious attention to them. In simplest terms, they become reflexes. Such reflexes are not easily uprooted. Attempted change usually results in varying degrees of uncertainty, discomfort, loss of confidence and devastating consequences to your quality of play. In short, in attempting stroke changes you are tinkering with dynamite! Some of you may be able to make some adjustments, but with **many** of you I suggest it is better to omit stroke changes and learn to use effectively the equipment you have.

A **second** question about stroke changes has two facets, both of which involve time. First, how much time do you have to practice with the new form so as to become comfortable with it? The great majority of people do not have unlimited time to spend on the court in drills. They are on tight schedules, and they usually want to play sets. The buddy with whom they play is likewise limited in time and is not likely to take kindly to being a backboard for a friend while said friend drills on new form. The other phase of the time element involves the instructor, if you have one. Is he/she able to check regularly with you to detect reversions to the old form? Seldom is this true, so you had better go along with your present form of strokes.

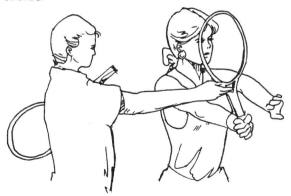

The **third** question involves the level of play at which you are competing. Most of you are playing at a social level. Your opponents likely have stroke weaknesses similar to yours. But neither stroke perfection nor considerable power is needed to hit the ball to various parts of the court. A match can be completely turned around by judicious ball placement, considering depth and angle for starters. Here you have a fertile field for improvement with little or no change in strokes or grips.

In summary, be careful about trying to change your strokes or grips. Such changes may work out fine or they may cause total confusion and loss of confidence. Judgment, not blanket application of standardized form, is required to convey the greatest benefits. Classic strokes do not necessarily produce winners. The judicious use of power and placement against THIS PARTICULAR opponent can do wonders, even if the strokes are unorthodox.

# REMEMBER LIMITING FACTORS

Much is written, videotaped, discussed, photographed and rehashed over "ideal" strokes in tennis. Many believe, "If I can acquire those perfect strokes, I'll be a winner." Not so, my dear player. Once you develop those perfect strokes, whatever they are, you will still be constrained by five limits in their use. Violations of any one of these limits will cause numerous unforced errors and a losing effort in match play. Here are those limits.

**First** and most important is FAILURE TO CONCENTRATE, failure to watch the ball long enough to hit the sweet spot with each stroke. The signal that you are not watching it long enough is off-center hits. Just as you must have physical endurance to last through the longest matches, so you must also have **concentration endurance** or a match can get away from you completely. Remember the 5-1, 30-love lead that suddenly became a 5-7 set lost? Your opponent rallied? No, you just "went out for a coke and sandwich" before the set was over. At 5-all you couldn't get your game back and lost the set. In a 6-2, 2-6, 6-2 match the sports page reports that the loser "rallied" in the second set. Nope! Another "out for coke and sandwich" case or, simply, lost concentration for one set. All else is fruitless unless you have concentration, sustained and intense, throughout the match.

The **second** limit on strokes is LATE PREPARATION and accompanying POOR POSITION. (Very likely a low level of concentration is also involved!) If you are to hit with power and/or accuracy you must prepare carefully for each stroke. Watch the ball right off your opponent's racket and turn your "ready" position to the side the instant you can determine the direction of your opponent's return. Take the racket back just off the tight hip (forehand). This is done with one movement. BE WAITING for the ball when it arrives.

If ready, hit deep or to the corners. If not ready, if not really "set" for a stroke—go defensive. Shorten your swing and aim to clear the net by five or six feet or more, hitting the ball deep, if possible, but KEEPING IT IN PLAY AT ANY COST! Also, watch for pet shots by your opponents; anticipating these will improve your preparation.

The **third** limit on strokes is attempting to hit with just a little TOO MUCH POWER for **you**. Control and consistency will be lost. If your power drives are shallow, the chances are the ball will come back with considerably more power than you hit it in the first place. Take a little less power and, instead, provide depth or angle. Either of these will cause many errors or weak returns which you can then attack.

The **fourth** limit on strokes is OVER-PLAYING, with the resulting faulty accuracy as you try to place the ball too close to the lines or to the top of the net. It is natural to want to hit the ball so far from your opponent that it is out of reach, but that attempt will usually result in one placement (or ace) and from four to ten errors on your part. If your opponent makes no errors at all, you would have lost two games and won only one point in a series like that. Your target should be no closer than four feet from the baseline or sidelines.

An additional suggestion regarding this fourth point is DO NOT TRY TO "PSYCH" YOURSELF UP for match play. That sort of thing sounds so good in print, but generally it does not work. You are likely to try to play TOO well, to overplay with both power and accuracy, and just blow yourself right out of the match. Play just as you do in practice, intensely, with determination.

The **fifth** limit on strokes is FEAR, fear that you cannot make the very good shot you want to make, fear that you cannot sustain rallies, fear of losing. Always accompanying fear is tension. You get "the elbow." Strokes that should be fluid become jerky. Control goes right down the drain. How do you overcome fear? First, You must learn in practice exactly what your capabilities are. How many strokes can you hit in succession and sustain a crisp rally without "moon-balling"? I find that very few players are keenly conscious of that important item, consistency. **Count** the total number of good strokes in five rallies or points. Are you averaging at least three, or better yet, five or six, or ten, if need be? If not, work on **steadiness** is badly needed. If you get into a match against a very consistent opponent who makes you hit the ball for more strokes than you are accustomed to making, that old fear of errors will tear your game apart.

How do you overcome the fear of losing? First, recognize that a period of losing usually precedes winning. In tournaments, you will likely draw top seeds at least by the second round and get "clobbered." Do your best, but expect a rough time for a while. Learn what you can from each match, and go home to practice, practice, practice. Art Andrews, one of my Iowa City youths, who was ranked No. 1 in the nation in junior singles and doubles, had the perfect attitude for match play. Said he, "If I lose that's just too darn bad, BUT I DON'T EXPECT TO LOSE!" Play tournaments or matches at every opportunity, and you will gradually overcome the fear of losing. Self-confidence will grow and you can approach the big matches with that same detached determination which Art so effectively employed.

# SERVE WITH THROWING MOTION

Natural tendencies play a very important role in earning the serve. Start at the baseline (very small children may begin at the service line) and imagine that you are going to throw your racket over the net, using an overhand throw—like a baseball pitcher. I emphasize the word "imagine" because a student once actually threw the racket over the net. If you ask me to demonstrate, I will do so with no explanations. DON'T THINK! Just throw.

The word "throw" is the key word or key concept which sets instinct in motion. Typically, you will take a step of moderate length with your left foot if you are right handed (right foot if left handed). As you take the step, you will swing your racket down past your right leg, backward and upward with a drop of the racket head behind your back, and finally carry it downward to follow through past your left leg in one smooth, continuous motion. I continue to marvel how many learners show me a service swing that is 65% to 90% perfect with their first try!

One likely variation from a perfect swing is a follow-through straight down or to the right of the right leg, rather than to the left of the left leg. Also, the racket head may not drop at the top of the swing as deep behind the back as it does with the experts. However, generally the service swing is initially correct. Usually I can build your confidence by showing you how very well you actually did on your first attempt.

Next, look at your grip. I recommend the Eastern forehand grip, which is attained by shaking hands with the handle when the face of the racket is in hitting position. That is, place the tip of the "V" formed by the thumb and index finger squarely above the top bevel of the handle. Grip close to the end of the handle. I strongly discourage the Western grip for a number of reasons, but chiefly because it produces only a flat serve. The recommended grip will nearly always produce a natural slice. A flat serve clears the net by a narrow margin and bounces just the right height to permit your opponent to return it with great glee.

On the other hand, the preferred slice serve clears the net by a very comfortable margin, curves down and out to the left, and then bounces shoulder height to the opponent.

Very few beginners will be able to use a Continental grip for serving, so I usually leave them with the Eastern forehand grip. However, I add a warning that the Continental grip is a must for advanced play. It can be learned later, if needed.

For proper positioning of the feet near the baseline, place the left foot (if right handed) just back of the baseline at a 45 degree angle to it. You must not touch the line. Place the right foot parallel to the baseline and a racket's width back from your front foot. Next, allow your racket and arm to swing from your shoulder, like the pendulum on one of those old grandfather clocks, free and easy, several times.

With your feet in position, place your racket out in front of your body at waist height, **with the left hand holding the ball in contact with the throat of the racket**. This specific position of the racket and tossing hand is extremely important. The service motion is a beautifully smooth and rhythmic motion, with all the movements blending into a continuous whole. A student once said to me at this point, "The serve has four parts..." I stopped her to say, "Whoa! There is only ONE PART to a serve—ALL of it." I cannot think of a better way of messing up a serve than to begin thinking "parts."

You have made the preliminary swings from the shoulder. Now make the complete swing to actually hit the ball. DON'T THINK! NEVER ASK WHEN to toss the ball. The timing of the toss is instinctive. Your first couple of attempts are likely to be a bit wild. You may feel as though you are chasing a black cat in a dark room on a foggy night. But after two or three attempts you will begin to acquire the **feel** of the whole motion. Your toss will improve, and you will gain confidence.

In making the swing you may sometimes find yourself stopping the racket at the bottom of the swing and then lifting it straight up, rather than continuing the motion backward and upward. If this occurs, go back to the preliminary full arm swing for several repetitions and then go back to the complete swing. Check your follow-through to see that it is to the left of your body. By the time you have repeated the serve fifteen to twenty times you will feel quite comfortable with it.

One part of the serve that is NOT instinctive is the height of the toss. You probably toss the ball too low. To correct this, reach up with the racket over your shoulder to full arm length with the racket face vertical and toward the net. The center of the racket in this raised position is the target for your toss. And, if a ball were to fall from the center of the racket, it would drop about a foot from your left toe and toward the net.

You may look at the target of the raised racket and ask, "That high?" I agree that it does indeed look very high, but watch me serve a couple of times. Notice that the ball is hit just as it reaches the top of its ascent. Bill Tilden one said, "Don't toss the ball up and hit it, rather, toss the ball INTO the racket." That lifted racket face represents the path of the racket at its highest point, and the ball MUST be tossed to that spot. **A serve can be no better than the toss**. If you make a bad toss, just catch the ball and start again. There is no penalty for making a bad toss and catching it, but if you swing at a poorly tossed ball, you use up (and often lose) that serve.

serving. It may come quite easily, or it may be difficult. How much time do you have to practice? What quality of competition do you face? To achieve the ultimate power with your serve the deep drop of the racket head to your shoulder blades is a must, but for average play you can get along with something less than that.

I do not like to use the word "toss" since it sounds like a flip or snap of the wrist. I prefer "lift" or "place" the ball to that measured spot. Take some practice lifts of the ball to your target without a swing. There is no short-cut to accurate tossing or lifting. It demands practice—practice—practice.

Now that your swing and toss are moderately successful, we look at control. If your racket face is rising when it contacts the ball, the serve will be long. If the toss is too far out in front of the body, the racket is descending and the ball goes into the net. Somewhere between those two points, along the arc made by the racket, is a point at which the tangent made by the flight of the ball takes the ball unerringly into the service court, a bit of plane geometry. Try a serve, noticing carefully the point of contact of racket and ball. Is the serve long? If so, the toss must be made farther forward. If the serve goes into the net, the toss must be moved back. Know exactly where your toss must go.

Generally, you do not drop the racket head behind your back as deeply as I prefer. If so, stop your racket at the top of the swing, and as the racket head is dropped, bring it against your body. Where does it strike your body? If your racket hits between your shoulder blades, great! More likely it strikes the back of your neck. Practice a deeper drop of the racket as you make the full swing, and then return to actually

**Placement** of your serve is your next objective, and placement is much more important than power. Learn to place the serve to the forehand, to the backhand, or one of the best serves, straight at your opponent. To assist you in practicing placement, use an actual **target** to aim for—a racket cover or whatever is handy. After a few tries, and with sustained concentration on your target as your focus, you will be hitting close to it. A direct hit is not necessary, but a pattern of close hits is your goal.

It is a matter of statistical fact that close to 60% of all strokes used in game play are either serves or returns of service. Think hard a moment! Three out of every five strokes in match play are either serves or returns of service. How can you realize the potential of these so-important strokes? Since few of us can enjoy the luxury of a bucket of balls with which to practice a service, here is your answer: **begin your practice rallies with a serve and return of service.**

Beginning practice rallies with a serve takes a little more time than hitting the ball out of your hand. However, when you consider that it takes little skill to hit the ball out of your hand and not much more skill to return that first ball, two strokes are wasted. You can see that time is actually saved and valuable practice gained by starting with a serve.

The serve is the only stroke in tennis over which your opponents have no control. They can only stand and wait for you to do as you wish. What an advantage, if you work to polish this all-important stroke! Remember, learn to **place** the serve first. Then, gradually apply power only as you can control it.

# ATTACK SHORT RETURNS

Tennis players I observe practicing groundstrokes often appear to be more or less anchored behind the baseline. They seem to treat short returns—balls that bounce near the service lines—as a nuisance. They take these "nuisance" balls on the second, third, or whatever bounce in violation of one of the basic fundamentals of tennis. "Get into position for stroking the ball on the first bounce." By taking the ball on other than the first bounce they miss an opportunity to attain a high degree of skill in this important fundamental.

Those who fail to take the ball on the first bounce also miss an opportunity to take advantage of a weak return for attack. Yes, ATTACK from the baseline in a two-stroke sequence. That is, the midcourt ball is taken on the first bounce and hit DEEP! By DEEP I mean within six feet of the baseline for the average player and within two feet for the advanced player. If this depth is attained with the midcourt shot, the second stroke of the sequence, a volley at the net, should be quite simple.

This attack pattern will be familiar to anyone who has seen high-quality tournament play by either men or women. **Watch eagerly** for the short return. **Go to** the ball on the first bounce. Hit it **deep**. Go on to the net! Maybe your volley isn't great but if the midcourt shot is deep, it won't need to be.

Let me say right here that this plan of attack is not reserved exclusively for advanced players. With a little consistent practice it can be just as effective for anyone, women as well as men. As one woman student eventually remarked: "At first I was scared to death to move into midcourt and then on up to the net. Now I feel so big up there!" And why not?

In attempting this midcourt stroke, also called an approach shot, you will feel very uncomfortable at first. One of the men remarked after his first lesson in which we emphasized this stroke, "Well, Coach, I understand what to do with the ball and I can see the value of the shot, but I don't feel comfortable in making it!" Incidentally, he made tremendous progress in just one session. No, you won't feel comfortable right away. After all, you are moving into "no man's land" and you have been told that is poisonous territory. It is no-no land if you **stay** there, but that midcourt shot is the golden opportunity for attack if it is played right.

I find that all of my players who are not familiar with the approach shot attempt it with a desperate fear of their opponent. They fear they will be passed, lobbed, and run right off the court! Oh, what the baseline opponent is going to do to them! I counter these fears with, "How do **you** feel when your opponent comes to the net? Can **you** pass well? Can **you** lob accurately?" And the answer in essence is: "Who, ME?" Right! Your opponent is in the same boat. Don't attribute abilities to your opponent which aren't there. Your approach shots won't have to be great because your opponent's strokes aren't either. So, let's go!

I have used the term "golden opportunity" for attack from the baseline in connection with this midcourt shot. It is the **key** effort in the two-stroke sequence. If it is hit well, the succeeding and climactic volley at the net should be simple. If it isn't hit deep or sharply angled, you may or may not be in trouble with the volley. Don't panic. You will recall that opponents also make poor shots and may set one right up for you.

The approach shot is not expected to earn a point by itself. If it does because you have hit an unusually good shot or because your opponents make an error, great! You have a one-stroke bonus. Its prime aim is to **force** your opponents so that they will give you a set-up volley at the net. You want it to be a forcing shot, not an ace. If you attempt to hit aces with it you will make far too many errors.

How do you make the approach shot forcing? Hit it DEEP, and generally with slice. As I said earlier, hit within two to six feet of the baseline, depending on the quality of play. In the early stages of work on the shot, concentrate on depth alone. Really aim for the baseline. If some of your shots go long, DO NOT let up on your attempts to go deep. You will gradually acquire the control to place the ball close to the baseline. If the approach shot is made on a bounce

at or below net height, it cannot be hit hard. Place it in a low trajectory deep to the baseline targets. If it bounces higher than the net, you will be able to put some extra zip on the ball.

Depth alone will make the shot forcing, but I like to think in terms of three specific targets: A) DEEP and in the forehand corner; B) DEEP and in the backhand corner; or C) DEEP and straight at your opponents. Targets A and B pull your opponents to the sides and leave the court wide open for your volley. Target C brings the ball straight at them, making it difficult to get into position for stroking and, in addition, reducing their angles for passing you at the net.

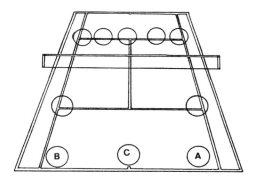

In working with players at all levels of ability, I seldom find ones who have learned to observe **where** their shots hit in their opponent's court and the **effect** that particular shot will have on their opponent's return. This is a **necessary** observation if you are to capitalize fully on the midcourt shot. If you hit hard but shallow, your opponents will likely stroke with confidence. But if you hit the ball DEEP or run them to either side, notice that many of their returns will be short. If you can EXPECT short returns, then you can make early preparation for going forward to the short ball and really playing an effective approach shot. Learn to watch the ball from your racket to its contact with your opponent's court. If it is DEEP, get set for the short return. If you don't learn to expect these shallow returns, you will be booby-trapped time and again by the effects on your opponents of your fine deep or wide shot. Heads up! Watch for that short return.

Here is a trick for sharpening your concentration. NEVER assume that the ball will come **to** you. Rather, assume that it may go anywhere in the court at any time. In combination with learning to observe the effects of your shots on your opponent, this little gimmick will have you off to meet the ball in a manner that will surprise you. Getting there a little sooner means better preparation and better position means more forcing shots.

How is the approach shot to be hit? Hit with whatever stroke that comes naturally to you. Top spin, flat, or slightly undercut can all be effective. If you have to hurry forward, you may find it difficult to use top spin since we generally hit this shot best from a sidewise position. If so, you may find the undercut shot easiest to employ. Power is not critical. Depth is! Recall that this shot is the key in **forcing** your opponent. It is not expected to win the point outright, although you will get many points from your opponent's errors. Keep in mind that your very presence at the net is a threat to your opponent even though you may not have too much confidence in your net play.

One might naturally assume that the midcourt shot could be made with ease, and with little practice. Not so! As you move into the court, the court length in effect becomes shorter. That is, if the approach shot is made from ten feet inside the baseline, you have only about seventy feet in which to keep your shot good. If it is made over the service line, that length decreases to sixty feet. Also, the net becomes relatively higher as you move forward toward it. Power must be reduced and the trajectory of the ball lowered. Take every opportunity you can find to practice on this shot.

While this "shortening" of the court presents some handicaps, it still forces your opponents because they have less time to prepare for such shots. Furthermore, as you move forward, the angles available to you become greater—not a great deal, but enough to add a bit more difficulty for your opponents. Yes, this midcourt shot is the key and it can be potent.

## AIM WELL ABOVE THE NET

Forehand and backhand drives directed to the opponent's baseline should clear the net by one and one-half to four feet. The idea that most of your shots should pass close to the top of the net is one of the most dangerous misconceptions in tennis! In case of excessive back spin hit hard, or shots off low bounces hit inside the baseline, the clearance will be less. On the other hand, top-spin shots will need increased clearance or they will not have depth. Try driving from the baseline and observe closely your net clearance and the depth of your shots. Note that those drives which look so pretty skimming the net are invariably

shallow, striking the court near the service line. Such drives, unless they have a wide angle have little offensive value even when hit very hard. More often they allow an opponent to attack.

One winter we conducted an experiment on net clearance in its relation to depth. The back courts were marked cross-wise into three zones, each six feet deep and twenty-seven feet wide. No. 1 Zone included a depth of six feet just behind the service line, and No. 3 Zone included the six feet of depth in front on the baseline, with No. 2 Zone between the other two. Above and parallel to the net we stretched chalk-lines. The first was one foot above the ends of the net, and one foot six inches above the net at the center. It was easy to check the approximate net clearance of the ball on each shot by means of these cords and to note the zone in which it landed on the court.

In the normal rallying of the subjects, no shots clearing the net by less than one and one-half feet landed farther back in the court than Zone 2, with nearly all such shots landing either in the service courts or in Zone 1. Most of them struck the court close to the service line. In order to achieve depth—defined as the back six feet of the court in this study, or Zone 3—the drives cleared the net mostly between the two- and four-foot levels. One of the subjects, using more than average top-spin, not at all excessive, was clearing the net by four and five feet on his deeper shots. Even when the boys were told to really blast 'em, we found that very few drives achieved the prime requisite, **depth**, unless the net clearance was more than one and one-half feet. This study wasn't guesswork nor was it subjective. Anyone could duplicate the test very easily.

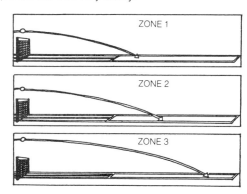

I know what your natural reaction is likely to be. Must be dink tennis! Try it yourself. Watch two factors carefully—the net clearance and the depth of each shot as you vary your power. If the drives are skimming the net they are almost certain to be shallow. Shallow drives are likely to be an invitation to your opponent to attack with a forcing drive, a drop shot, or a decisive shot from mid-court on the way to the net.

The misconception that net-skimming shots are good tennis often arises from a situation such as this: two players are hitting the ball hard, clearing the net by a foot or less, their drives landing in the vicinity of the service line. Shots such as these are perfect set-ups for the opponent to drive hard, too; hence, there is a pretty rally, pretty if it isn't analyzed in the light of winning tennis matches. At the end of the rally the players and the spectators heave a sigh: "Boy, what a rally!" But why provide your opponents with a perfect opportunity to drive? Any player who prefers a hard-driving game likes to have his opponent hit hard, and shallow, too. Shallow drives provide the opponent with plenty of time to get set and the height of the bounce will be just right at the baseline for a perfect drive in return. If you are trying to win, however, you must put your opponent at a disadvantage, not set 'em up for him! Depth, please, depth! And depth calls for adequate net clearance, one and one-half feet or more.

There is a danger from net-skimming even greater than that of being kind to your opponent with shallow drives. That is the danger of net errors. No one has pin-point accuracy, least of all the average or better-than-average players. Let's consider this statistical problem for a moment. Across a smooth wall draw a line two inches in width at a height of three feet six inches above the floor. You are to rally the ball against the wall, attempting to hit the line anywhere over its entire length. From the law of averages you could expect approximately 50% of your shots to strike above the line and 50% below it. Of the 50% of shots falling below the three feet six inches height, probably forty out of fifty will be six inches or more below the line. But the net height at the center is six inches below target line and only about one inch less at the sidelines. This leaves you with at least 40% of your total strokes as net errors if you are aiming your shots close to the top of the net. Since many balls are hit off-center on the racket, resulting in loss of power and distance, this figure is conservative. Sounds a bit like "figures don't lie, but liars do figure," doesn't it? But let's consult error analysis charts. Rallies in match play seldom average over two and one-half strokes per player. Errors commonly constitute 75% and up of all points played in average tennis. Of the total errors in average play, **net** errors make up approximately 67%, long errors amount to about 21%, and wide errors approximately 12%. From a strategic viewpoint, the long and net error percentages should be reversed in an attempt to attain depth. Fine players will tell you they don't worry if their drives tend to be a little long; but they are seriously concerned if they are netting very many shots. And they **should** be concerned. As I have shown, your shots will have plenty of net clearance if aimed for depth. Hence few of your drives should result in net errors. You can afford to drive some of them over the baseline in order to attain depth.

How can you get away from net error? First, revise your conception of beautiful drives. Don't evaluate them on their closeness to the top of the net, but on their depth or angle. Forget the net! It's **poison!** Aim for the baseline, not for the top of the net.

Now the changing of habits—physical, mental, or emotional—can be, and usually is, a trying, exasperating, and often frustrating proposition. When habit and logic clash, logic is likely to take a beating. Even when you understand the situation fully, physical habit will likely pull you back to net-skimming, unconsciously at first. Have patience! Watch the effect of depth on your opponent. You will see endless errors and weak returns resulting from your depth. A ball doesn't have to be hit very hard if it is deep or angled. On the other hand, as I have shown, speed has little value if it is shallow. So let's worship at the alter of depth rather than at the shrine of net-skimming drives. The latter should make you shudder rather than exult.

Secondly, use the baseline as your point of aim, **not the top of the net**. Hit **through** the ball to the limit. You will get adequate net clearance automatically.

Easily? I didn't say that. The touch required for driving with sustained depth calls for hard, conscientious effort. You will have to hit hundreds and thousands of shots, going all-out to lay that ball close to the baseline. At least the champions have to learn it this way. Can you expect to attain the skill with less effort? Rest assured the results to be gained are worth it.

# TAKE ADVANTAGE OF THE HIGH BOUNCE

Tennis players usually fail to take advantage of the high bounce: either they make a weak return from the top of the bounce or back up and let the ball fall to waist height. In both cases, an opportunity has been lost to make a forcing shot. With the ball so high above the net, it can be hit **down** into the opponent's court, a geometric advantage that should not be passed up.

I stumbled on a very simple approach to learning this shot. I call it the "timing method." Concentrate on one item—namely, the contact between ball and racket at a point even with the shoulder nearest the net. Give no thought as to "how" to hit the ball, no attention at all to form. Concentrate entirely on "when."

To work on this shot, place yourself at one service line, assuming the side-to-net positions you would use for a drive stroke. Have a friend take a position at the opposite service line and toss the ball underhand very accurately so that it reaches you at the top of the bounce and approximately shoulder high. Go easy on power; there is a tendency to swing too hard at first. Concentrate on timing only.

Since people vary considerably in their reactions to any one technique, a correction may have to be made on the exact point of contact. If the ball is being hit down and to the left with the forehand, contact

is being made too soon. If it is going high and to the right, contact is too late. Within a dozen or so strokes, you will be able to determine the exact point of contact of ball and racket.

The ball may be stroked flat, it may be slightly undercut, or it may be hit with topspin. Since the ball is so high above the net it doesn't really matter which method is used. Each individual will make an automatic selection without prompting. This shortens the learning time dramatically.

Once you begin stroking the ball with confidence at the service line, have your friend hit the ball to you from the baseline; then away from you so that you get the feel of hitting the stroke from all areas of the court. Develop accuracy before applying too much power.

A short drill on this stroke must be included in each practice session until it becomes habitual. Once that level of performance is achieved, each high bounce in match play will be accepted as an opportunity to gain points with forcing shots placed into the opponent's court as the situation may warrant.

# MOVE FORWARD

It has been traditional to rally from the baseline until the opponent makes a short return, then go to midcourt, hit the ball deep and go on to the net for the volley. This is indeed a sound approach. I would add a refinement to this strategy. Learn to **read** your offensive returns according to their forcing quality. If you have made a high quality forcing shot, at least move well inside the baseline ready to approach the net according to the return. If you read your shot as severely forcing, go all the way to the net immediately. The concentration involved is intense and the judgment must be good or you can be in a bit of trouble. Properly applied, this technique is exciting and pays off in many winning points.

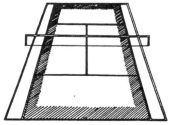

Take note of the accompanying singles court diagram. The shaded areas around the edges of the court are approximately four feet wide. Crisp drives hit into these shaded areas are very likely to be forcing against the average player. As you go up the scale in ability the quality of your forcing shot will have to be higher, but the possibility is still there.

If your shot is forcing, there will be one of three results with great regularity. First and most commonly, the return will go into the net. The second possibility will be a very short return just over the net. And the third possibility will be a rather high, slow floater. None of these responses is intentional, rather, just the result of being forced. Since you can predict these results with a high degree of certainty, the logical conclusion would be that you should at least go well inside the baseline ready to move forward. If the ball goes into the net, no problem. If the return is very short, you can pounce on it for a put-away. If you had remained behind the baseline, you would be booby-trapped by the result of your own fine shot. If the ball comes back high, you should have an easy volley to hit before your opponent has time to recover. If you read your shot as being severely forcing, you should go all the way to the net at once.

There are three requirements for this plan of attack to be successful, none of which is easy to acquire. The first requirement is concentration, intense and sustained. The ball must be watched intently to its point of contact with the opponent's court. Obviously, a shot that is more than four feet from the baseline or the sideline will not be as forcing as one within a foot of the lines. In the early stages of learning to watch the shot closely, you will often go forward on shots that are not forcing enough, but with time and practice your judgment will become very accurate.

The second skill to be acquired is to observe the effect of the forcing shot on your opponents. This will vary with opponents and with their degree of skill. It is not so important whether your opponent's **make** a return from your forcing shot, but the **quality** of the return. For instance, they may make many errors as a result of your deep drives or they may just block them back defensively, rather high above the net. Such returns are set-ups for a good volleyer. The skill required here is the ability to evaluate your opponent's return.

The third skill needed is the ability to volley or half-volley with confidence with any return from low to just short of the overhead. For returns at or above net height I'd encourage you to swing volley, going for power more than accuracy. For the high ones, hit short angles. If the return is low, play it back DEEP and move to the net.

When tennis players attempt to lob over a net rusher, they frequently hit the ball down the line or straight down the center of the court. Pythagoras, who antedated the origin of tennis by several generation gaps and who would have loved the game, discovered the relationship between the sides of a right triangle. In simple terms, the hypotenuse (diagonal side) of a right triangle is always longer than either of the other two sides. Since this is true, there is more margin for lobs hit **crosscourt** than lobs hit down the line. Elementary, my dear Watson.

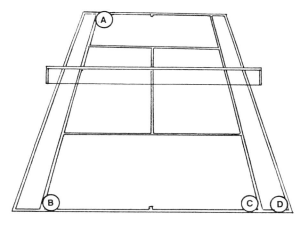

FROM A TO B = 80 feet
FROM A TO C = 84 ft. 5 in.
FROM A TO D = 87 ft. 9 in.

Consider what can occur when lobs are hit from two feet back of the baseline corner, singles or doubles, as the case may be. If the lob is hit down the line, it can go no further than 80 feet and still be good. If the net rushers are eight feet from the net, they would have to move back 23 feet to cover the best down-the-line lob in singles or doubles. If the lob is hit crosscourt in singles, it can travel up to 84'5" and still be good, and the net player will have to cover 26'4" to reach it.

In doubles the lob hit from two feet back of the corner can travel 87'9", and the net player will have to move 28'6" to reach it. The lob can be 4'5" longer in singles, 7'9" longer in doubles, hit crosscourt vs. down the line.

If you would like to have geometry, mathematics, effectiveness and statistics on your side, use the **crosscourt** lob.

# CHAPTER SIX
# PRACTICE EFFECTIVELY

## WARM UP GRADUALLY

All through the warm-up, take it easy! From the viewpoint of physical safety, **there should be no hard hitting, particularly of serves or overheads until a player is thoroughly warmed up.** The warm-up should include plenty of practice on these two strokes, as well as ground strokes and volleys, but it is possible to injure seriously the shoulder muscles, sometimes permanently, by just one hard swing while those muscles are still cold. I repeat, ground strokes do not completely warm up the muscles used in hitting a serve or an overhead, so go easy on them until you know the warm-up is complete.

The same principle applies to hard running or to quick stops or starts. **Just don't do it** until you are thoroughly warmed up. The risk is too great. You may violate this physiologic principle many times without penalty, only to find yourself suddenly handicapped severely with badly torn leg muscles. Your luck in playing too hard too soon may not last forever.

Cold muscles will not respond smoothly, so stroke easily at first. Use half speed or less hitting the ball down the middle of the court and not too deep. Your opponent isn't warmed up either.

Yes, I know you are full of zip and rarin' to go. So what do you do? You begin your practice session swinging as though your warm-up is over and you are in full playing condition. Strokes are hit wildly into the net and out of bounds. If you do get the ball over, your opponent flubs it. There is no concentration, just hitting. The exhilaration of blasting away quickly dissipates while you work yourself into a state of frustration and then have to settle down to take it easier until you do become adequately warmed up. Let's take it easy **first** and then gradually increase pace, depth, and angle as you become warmed up.

Few players think of the warm-up as being a mental as well as a physical thing. Actually, the nervous system needs to warm up to the tasks to which you will subject it, just as the muscles do. Don't ask your nervous system to assume a heavy load until it is gradually adjusted to the performance expected of it. Your timing will be poor at first. Timing, vision, concentration must not be overlooked. They too need a warm-up. Take it easy! Give all of your body systems a chance to adjust themselves to playing tempo.

Sustained concentration is so important. Without it no player can ever attain and hold a high level of performance. Easy now! Concentration requires a warm-up too! With the very first stroke of the practice period let's get our mind on what we are trying to do with the ball. Don't put yourself under a severe mental strain by attempting to hit too well, that is, too accurately or too hard. You simply won't be up to it and the inevitable result will be a pathetic succession of errors. Sustained concentration, like physical condition, is a result of continual training, a mental conditioning, which must be worked at diligently in **every** practice. Go to work on it from the first stroke in the warm-up. Instead of just hitting the ball in the general direction of the opposite court, aim it to your opponent's forehand or backhand, and not too deep at first. Now **follow it to your opponent's racket and back.** Be set for the ball when it reaches you. Now place it to the backhand. Repeat the whole process throughout your warm-up, and your practice session, too. Easy! You are full of ginger and want to blast away? Yes, I know, but you aren't warmed up, physically or mentally. Neither is your opponent. Save your energy for a few minutes. We will be going at it **hard and fast** soon enough. You won't learn sustained concentration with rallies of two strokes or less. Build habits of steadiness through concentration. Be steady in your warm-up. Make it **habitual.** Steadiness gives a sense of control, a security that is a joy to possess.

Another habit to develop with painstaking care is that of playing within your ability. If you over-hit during the warm-up, you are simply training yourself to over-play your game all of the time. How can you tell that

you are overhitting? Simple! Your rallies will end in errors with less than three strokes per player in each rally.

To learn effectively, the difficulty of the task must be adjusted to, or very little beyond, the ability of the learner. Overload will only result in a breakdown of the learning process. Hence, if you begin your rallies with shots that are going way out at the start of the warm-up, you are overloading. Such a procedure is wasted time. It is not purposeful, intelligent practice. The same shots that you will miss at the beginning of the warm-up can probably be executed with ease after the warm-up is complete. Build up slowly to your normal game by hitting within your ability.

To summarize, no one's body systems are in tune for intense effort until they are adequately warmed up. Demands on muscles, circulatory and nervous systems must be very light at first. The tempo of practice is slowly increased as you become adjusted to more difficult performances through the warm-up. Forcing the muscles beyond their capacity during the warm-up period invites injury. Attempting to stroke too well during the warm-up contributes to poor concentration and tends to develop the habit of over-playing your strokes, two cardinal sins of tennis players. As you practice so will you play in matches. In match play we depend on habits developed in practice. Carefully nurture in the warm-up those habits that will help you gain the greatest number of points in match play.

## BEGIN WITH A SERVE

Probably the oldest maxim in sports is, "You should practice as you expect to play in competition." Simple and sound!! Practice patterns should be carefully planned to build in you, the player, the conditioned reflexes on which you must depend in match play.

Traditionally in tennis, up to 85% of practice time is spent on groundstrokes made from back of the baseline. The players will take the ball on the second or third bounce, if necessary, in order to maintain this behind-the-baseline position. While it is definitely desirable to develop good groundstrokes and it is unquestionably fun to hit them, as an analyst of the game I must ask if groundstrokes merit that much attention. And a second pertinent question, "How long can ANYONE work profitably on any one stroke?" Isn't there a real danger that after your optimum time you will become careless and tend to break down the desirable mechanics that should be developed during the effective portion of the practice session?

Intensive charting of tennis matches shows that the total strokes per point seldom average more than four. In the televised matches one season, the average was approximately 3.2 strokes per point. For simplicity take an average of four. The first stroke will always be a serve, the second stroke a return of service, the third stroke will depend on whether the server remains on the baseline or goes to the net. If you go to the net, the third stroke will be a volley or half-volley, and the fourth will be a passing shot or a lob. If you stay on the baseline, the third and fourth strokes will likely be groundstrokes. At any rate, 25% of the rally will consist of a service and 25% will be a return of service, or a total of 50% of all the strokes used in match play! The implications for the design of your practice patterns are obvious. Traditional practice systems are sadly inadequate to contend with the stroke situations you will face in match play!

You may ask, "But aren't the return of service and a passing shot both groundstrokes?" Indeed, each one is; but a serve may come with all degrees of spin, slice-twist or topspin, whereas the customary beginning stroke is hit flat or with very little topspin. The return of service also calls for a block, a chip, or a slice return as well as the drive return. A full swing will be very inadequate in returning some types of service.

The passing shot is indeed also a groundstroke, but the psychological situation is vastly different from that encountered when rallying from the baseline. Many passing shots should be hit so that they will strike the court near the service line so that the net player must volley up. This shallow return is just what **shouldn't** be hit if your opponent is on the baseline.

The only effective way to learn to hit good passing shots is to place your opponents near the service line and then to hit mostly shallow drives to right, left, or at their feet. Baseline driving simply won't get the job done.

After a great deal of experimentation, I believe that the only practical way to learn to serve and return service is to begin rallies with serves and returns of service. Serving practice with a bucket of balls may be helpful, but it's not necessary. Here are some guiding points for implementing the plan for beginning rallies with a service:

1. EITHER player begins each rally with a serve rather than hitting the ball out of your hand.

2. Serve from ANYWHERE along the baseline. Do not necessarily go to a fixed spot as you do in match play.

3. Indicate to your opponents to which point you intend to serve, i.e. outside corner, inside corner, or straight at them. In practice you aren't trying to ace anyone, but to put the ball in play toward one of three targets so that your opponent will have a good opportunity to return the service. Generally, select a CONVENIENT target for them. If they happen to be in the middle of the court, aim for one of the inside corners, for instance. If they are near the alley, aim for the outside corner.

4. Attempt to return all serves, in or out. A long serve is just as good for practice on return of service as a legal serve.

5. Hit the return of service directly back to your opponents or indicate to them where you intend to hit it, so that they may go to that point and continue the rally.

6. Continue the rally after the return of service, just as you would normally do.

7. Receivers do not necessarily go to the standard receiving position each time. Take the return of service as may be convenient for you at the conclusion of the rally. Receivers can help the server with practice to the outside corners by staying directly behind those corners after retrieving balls near the sides of the court.

8. DO NOT make endless serves into the net! Those shots benefit no one. A long serve is at least good practice for the receiver.

9. To repeat, EITHER player may begin the rally with a serve just as you now begin rallies by either player hitting the ball out of hand.

Beginning the rallies with a serve will take a little more time than hitting the ball out of your hand. However, when you consider that it takes little skill to hit the ball out of your hand and not much more to return that first ball, two wasted strokes, then time is really saved by starting with a serve.

As one could logically expect, the quality of serve and return of service will improve dramatically, especially the return of service. As your confidence in the return of service increases, begin stepping inside the baseline to hit the ball, especially on the softer second serve. Go to meet the service, hitting it to either corner or back at the server's feet. Keep the return DEEP! Then if you have a decent volley, go on in to the net and kill the weak return. NO PLAYER AT ANY LEVEL OF PLAY SHOULD EVER BE ALLOWED TO GET BY WITH AN EASY SECOND SERVE!! And they won't if the return of service is allotted the practice time it deserves.

# PRACTICE VOLLEYS NATURALLY

In match play the volley usually follows an approach toward the net, either behind service or after a shot from mid-court, when your opponent has made a shallow return. The first volley may be made from close to the service line, and then you should move closer to the net after each successive volley, depending on your opponent's tendency and ability to lob.

Note that no fixed position is taken for the volley. You do not automatically stop ten to twelve feet from the net and do all your volleying from that point. You **volley and move in** as far as you dare, **maybe all the way to the net**, to take advantage of the much greater angle into which you can volley when close to the net. Furthermore, the closer you can get to the net, the less opportunity your opponent will have of making you volley **up** defensively. A ball that must be volleyed upward from twelve feet back can be volleyed downward if you are at the net.

But what is the customary procedure in volley practice? Players take a fixed position about ten to twelve feet from the net. They expect the balls to be hit directly to them so that they don't ever get practice on moving laterally, let alone forward. It is strictly an artificial situation, not one designed to develop cagey, forcing net play. Getting to the net area may be a handicap rather than an advantage if you remain too far from the net. Your opponent can make you volley up defensively by hitting low around your ankles, and then either move in to midcourt to take your rising volley for a put-away, or easily pass you from the baseline. In addition, you will have only a very narrow angle for your volley, one which your opponent can cover easily.

Make your volley practice as **natural** as possible by following one of three plans. First, serve and come to the net immediately. Or second, begin rallying from the baseline, but take the first short return for an approach shot, followed by volleys, moving ever closer to the net. Isn't there a danger of being lobbed? Certainly! But learn to judge when your opponent will lob or try to pass you and play accordingly.

A third method of making volley practice more natural is to begin at the service line and gradually work forward from there. I prefer either of the other two plans, but at least this is better than anchoring yourself at one position. Encourage your opponent to attempt to pass you after a couple of strokes. Make this practice natural, the way you will be playing in a match.

It is obvious that practice should slowly develop and refine those habits of stroking and ball placement on which you can depend in match play. Logically then, every stroke in practice should contribute to the refining process. Does the customary practice pattern with the volley meet these standards? Definitely not!

In the usual procedure for practice on the volley, the player volleys short. That is, the ball will strike the court somewhere near the service line. Apparently the aim is to provide the baseline opponent with a very convenient shot to hit! The baseliner obligingly returns the ball sharply, chest high so that the net player can volley short, so that the baseliner can return the ball chest high, ad infinitum. This pattern is followed religiously and with great glee. Apologies follow immediately after a deep volley or an accidental passing shot. Are these the shots on which you must depend in match play? A volley that is a set-up to be handled as the baseliner sees fit? A return from the baseliner that asks to be put away by any decent player? The whole thing looks like a mutual assistance pact!

In match play you are out to win, of course. At the net you must **force** with your volleys. To be forcing they must be crisply hit (not blasted), and they must be deep—within six feet of the baseline—and generally into the corners. Define your targets by placing some object at each corner, five feet in each way from the sideline and the baseline. If you think that volleying within six feet of the baseline is easy, mark off a strip and try it. Do not expect a score of over six to eight good shots out of 25 attempts at first. Consistent practice will raise your score.

The practice system I like to use goes like this. Suppose the baseliner begins the rally with a stroke which hits the ball directly to the net player but low. The net player volleys straight back but deep. Or the net player begins the rally with a volley deep to the baseline, and the baseliner returns the ball low but close to the net player. In either case, after the second stroke, anything goes! The net player aims for a corner and deep. The baseliner tries to pass or lob. Play errors if you can reach them, just to work in all the stroking possible. Do not be afraid to volley many shots long in the early part of your practice. The baseliner should play them for good. After a time, both players should do their best to keep the ball in the court and still hit well. However, after the first two strokes, set-ups are put away without fail. Set-ups should never be missed (but average players miss them often).

Note how closely this practice system resembles match play after the first two strokes. Even those first two strokes are not played carelessly and will contribute their share to habit formation for competitive play. The remainder of the rally is still practice but under match play conditions.

## ALLOW NO SECOND BOUNCES

Two fundamentals of tennis are sustained concentration and good position for the stroke. Concentration involves watching the ball until it is almost to your racket, over and back again as long as the rally lasts.

Which comes first, the egg or the hen? In tennis, concentration is the egg, the chick, and the hen. Without it, forget all the rest.

The elements of good position are feet apart, knees bent, sidewise orientation to net, and the racket taken part way back as the ball approaches. It is interesting that even a beginner, when asked to pose for the forehand, will almost exactly duplicate this position without instruction. The mechanics of the human body are such that a player can hardly miss hitting the ball over the net and into the court, if he can assume good position for each stroke. Poor position sharply reduces accuracy, power, and consistency.

In match play there can be no second bounces. Logically, then, in practice take the ball on the first bounce or on the volley, unless it is completely out of reach. Go to the ball, don't let it take a second, third, or fourth bounce. Do not end a rally if the ball goes out of bounds. A drive that lands out is just as good for practice as one that lands in.

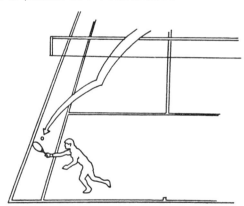

Another reason for playing shots that are out of bounds is to strive for sustained concentration. Few players can sustain their stroking for more than two or three shots. Poor concentration is the basic cause of this inconsistency. Mental endurance is as important as physical endurance.

Don't anchor yourself behind the baseline. Move forward to the ball rather than reaching for it. Reaching is almost certain to result in a weak error into the net or, at best, an ineffective return.

If you have bad practice habits, you will have to overcome a strong tendency to continue in that pattern, even though the logic is obvious. At first you may be disappointed, because you will find that you have less ability to get into good position than you had imagined. But you will now be conscious of good vs. bad position, not to mention lapses of concentration. However, there will be a steady improvement in both position and concentration if you bear down hard. As a consequence, your percentage of forcing returns will pick up remarkably. Paralleling this improvement will be increased self-confidence, the golden asset that can raise your entire game.

# PRACTICE PURPOSEFULLY

Three critical elements of purposeful practice were explained in the preceding three sections. Now, put these points together into a general practice pattern that will be very fruitful in developing the tennis you will use in your matches. You are now warmed up thoroughly and can run or hit as hard as you wish without danger of injury. From now on anything goes in all your rallies. That is, you can force each other and put away shots as the opportunity arises. Each rally is played as if it were a point in a match, but you do not keep score. Now suppose you begin the rally with a serve to the outside corner of the right service court. If you stay at the baseline, your opponents should try to hit their shots deep to keep you there. They will probably hit a few of their drives long in developing the touch for hitting close to that baseline. Of course, both players should attempt to return those long out-of-court shots. Keep that ball in play if you can reach it. You would have had to stroke under the same conditions if the ball had been a few inches shorter and in the court.

As soon as a return drops short, either player will move in. Don't avoid these short returns by taking second bounces. **Look** for them! They are golden opportunities for forcing your opponents and getting to the net where you can earn a point with a sharp volley. Do not try to **ace** your opponents with this approach shot, just force them. Keep it deep and usually into the corners, about six feet in the court each way from the baseline and side line. You will be passed now and then, but you should win well over half these points.

**This mid-court shot in coming to the net is one of the key strokes in tennis**. It must be played well or you leave yourself wide open to be passed or lobbed right out of a point. The shot becomes more difficult than a drive from the baseline because you are hitting the ball into a court which is, in effect, 12 to 18 feet shorter since you have moved in that far

from the baseline. Also, you are playing with the ball over a net that is relatively higher, since you are closer to it. Furthermore, you will be under stiff psychological pressure in knowing that you must hit well. If the approach shot is weak, you are in danger of being badly forced by your opponents. At the same time, if you try to hit too well, you merely force yourself into endless errors. Playing this mid-court approach shot effectively requires all the experience you can get. You can expect only a few clean placements from it, so it must be planned to force your opponents into weak returns often enough that you can win over half the points. Don't be disturbed by being frequently forced or passed by your opponents' returns so long as you are gaining the greater number of points as a result of your net attack.

If you approach too close to the net, won't your opponents lob over you? I don't know. **Can** they? **Will** they? Maybe they can seldom lob beyond the service line. Or perhaps they think that lobs are sissy stuff for only the "pushers." If they **can** and **will** lob, you will come in very close to the net only when you feel sure they won't be able to lob effectively, or when you have them forced and you think they are still going to try a passing shot. Such judgment is developed through daily practice.

When you go to the net you are helping your opponents to learn to change their stroking from hitting deep to the short type of shot which you just selected for a net attack from your position on the baseline. That same shot will now be dropping low around your feet, making you hit defensive half-volleys and giving you those mean low volleys which lead to errors or weak returns.

As mentioned earlier, under the usual practice pattern the baseliners hit set-ups to the net person by continuing to drive deep. Deep drives will clear the net by about three feet. How nice for you at the net! What the players at the baseline should learn to do is to suddenly change from deep to shallow driving. They need this shot against a net attack in singles, and they are hitting it constantly in doubles since their opponents should be coming to the net behind every service. How better can you learn it than by beginning practice rallies with serves and either following the serve to the net or moving in toward the net as soon as a drive falls short?

Whenever a set-up occurs, **put it away**! How often have you missed set-ups or seen them missed, these golden opportunities, at critical points in match play?

Learn to hit them well enough to win them outright, but not over-hit, and thereby increase your chances of missing. Are there exceptions in practice to putting away set-ups? Of course, but not many.

Practice is a teamwork proposition. Don't feel bad when you are passed at the net or your opponents drop a beauty at your feet and you flub it as you come in, or they float a beautiful lob over your head. By coming into mid-court you gave them the opportunity to learn a shot like that. Won't it look great to see them doing that to your opponents in doubles matches at tournaments later? You can pat yourself on the back. You helped them acquire that shot. You are teaching each other to volley, half-volley, lob, and hit overheads with great skill.

The point I want to emphasize is that you are now practicing exactly as you play in matches, with some concessions to keep the ball in play. Yet it is still a **practice** situation without the penalty of lost points to frighten you back into your old grooves that keep you from learning new strokes. As much as possible, play under the situations which will arise in match play.

Let's review this practice pattern that can help you develop a sound game you can depend on in match play. First, begin the rallies with serves, returning the serve, whether in or out, if it can be reached. The server will remain on the baseline for a while. Both players rally for depth, and angle, too, if they like. Run each other, but emphasize depth to keep each other away from the net. Early in the practice period return your opponent's long shots, if you can. Later, do your best to keep them all in the court. Sustained concentration! No second bounces, of course!

As soon as either of you hits short, the opponent should move in, make the approach shot, and go to the net. Now the one on the baseline must generally stop hitting deep and begin to hit short to keep the ball low at the net player's feet or execute a passing shot. If the net player gets in too close or you are forced by a good volley, lob for the back 12 feet of the court. This gives the baseliner lobbing practice and the net player a chance to work on his overhead. When you get a set-up, put it away as carefully as if it were match point.

For a period during the practice players should follow **all** of their serves to the net. This is just the practice players need for an effective return of service against a net rusher on one hand and a net attack behind a serve on the other.

Play a couple of sets in which you consistently apply the skills on which you have been working. Put yourselves under actual match conditions. You might agree for the first set that both players will come to the net on their first serve, or both serves. In the second set the players might do as they like. Slowly temper those new skills with the fire of competition. I have been asked if it is sometimes better to lose practice matches while learning something new, in order to bring this new phase of your game up to an effective level for match conditions. Definitely so, providing you are also learning to win with what you **have** rather than constantly losing while striving for something which you **want**. In tennis, as in life, while your are constantly trying to improve, you must play the match today according to your **present** abilities rather than according to your dreams or wishes.

Plan your practice sessions. Concentration on specific weaknesses results in rapid improvement. Whether you are a nine-year-old beginner or a college varsity player, progress comes most rapidly when you practice the same way that you play matches. In other words, practice purposefully.

# BUILD EFFORT AND CONCENTRATION

"Practice makes perfect!" is a slogan you can find almost anywhere. In essence, it means that faithful effort is required to achieve a high degree of skill. The fact remains, however, that practice **does not** make perfect! A boy with whom I was working the other day told me that he practiced six hours a day.

"Norm," I replied, "I'm afraid you are **on the court** six hours a day, but not **practicing properly** during most of that time. For instance, you are extremely late in 'getting set' for each stroke. Apparently, your method of 'practice' has done a fine job of 'making imperfect' preparation for your strokes.

"You should be watching the ball right off your opponent's racket so that you can begin preparation for your next shot at the earliest possible moment; but you seldom begin moving into position before the ball has passed the net. Then you attempt a long, high backswing when actually you have time for only a very short backswing, if any. Day by day the bad habit is becoming more and more firmly established."

No, practice doesn't necessarily make perfect. Not unless (1) the particular phase of the game which you're practicing is done in good form; (2) intense and sustained concentration on the task is maintained; and (3) the length of the practice period is limited to your ability to use it profitably.

Let's examine these three items one at a time. First, you should be striving toward form that is mechanically sound. How are you to know whether you're practicing in good form? The best answer is to have your performance observed by a competent coach, an established tennis professional, or a fine player who knows tennis thoroughly and can also teach it. There's just no satisfactory substitute for an overseer who's available day after day for help on your tennis problems.

The next best thing is to read, see movies, or watch fine players carefully. Stand in front of a mirror and observe yourself. You may be able to analyze and evaluate well enough by yourself, but it is likely to be a long, tiring and often frustrating process. If you get into a great deal of tournament play, other players will help you. Be on the alert to learn.

Analyze your own game as you practice. Many points lend themselves easily to simple and careful observation. For instance, do you find your weight on your front foot after each stroke?

Are you sidewise to the net most of the time on ground strokes?

Are you using muscles on your ground strokes or swinging the racket smoothly?

How often is your first serve coming into the court?

How many shots out of ten can you hit in any particular area of the court?

What is your percentage on overheads?

How many lobs can you hit into the back twelve feet of the back court?

Are you moving into position before the ball has passed your opponent's service line?

How many times out of each five strokes are you really "set" for the shot?

You don't need experts to evaluate such simple performances for you. They may be able to help you with the mechanics involved, but you can do such simple observations for yourself. You can measure your progress quite satisfactorily, too, by percentages such as these.

Second, concentration, **sustained** concentration, like all our other skills can be developed by day-after-day effort just as running endurance can be developed. It requires mental and physical effort. Half-hearted effort will get as its reward "half-baked" results. Generally speaking, we get what we pay for.

Mental "muscle" like physical muscle can be built to amazing strength by regular and purposeful practice. All great players have been masters of concentration, regardless of their strokes, footwork, or style of game. Cut out idle conversation once your practice drill begins. Put your mind exclusively on the job at hand. You can be positive that it can be done.

You can be certain that you won't get the job done in one day, one week, or one year. Progress will be steady for you, however, if you're willing to pay the price all great performers have paid—HARD WORK!

Let me warn you emphatically that you will need plenty of patience and determination to show improvement in your ability to keep your mind intently on your practice, to concentrate. It requires mental effort, something to which most players seem to show a very high natural resistance.

I base most of my teaching on an intense concentration by the player **on a point of aim for each shot**. The results are often spectacular, to say the least. But what a problem it is for me to secure that intense and sustained concentration from them! So I know what kind of struggle you're facing without a coach to incessantly encourage, inspire, and drive you to a higher level of achievement.

The proper amount of time to be spent on any item is something you can determine quite well for yourself. How long shall you work on a forehand drive just for depth, for instance?

Most of you have wrist watches or else your opponent will have one. Take note of the starting time for practice on this forehand drive for depth. Work hard, now! Just a forehand drive for depth, not six other items included, and no idle visiting while you are hitting. **Concentrate!** You should be able to go much longer than ten minutes on a single item, of course, but can you? I doubt it!

What about cross-court forehand, and backhands

down the line next? Ten minutes? I hope you can, but once more, I doubt it. The ability to sustain effort and concentration can be built by regular and conscientious practice. It develops just like running endurance, but **you have to work for it!**

The third point I want to make is that you shouldn't continue to hit any one shot or practice any one item or patterns of shots much beyond the time at which your interest will lag. When the practice becomes dull, go hard for a couple of minutes more and then go to work on something else. In this way you can gradually build the ability to sustain effort.

It is possible, of course, to combine two or three items in one practice drill. For instance, begin the rally with a serve and then rally for depth until one of you hits short. Then move in to attack at the net. This leads to an opportunity to pass and lob. But don't include too many items in drill or you won't derive the benefit that comes from many immediate repetitions of any one item.

All great performers in any area of life have been drill masters. This goes for coaches, too. All highly successful coaches are demons for drill until fundamentals are letter perfect. When your interest in practice begins to lag, go hard for another five minutes, and then play sets—but drive hard to increase the length of a profitable practice period day by day.

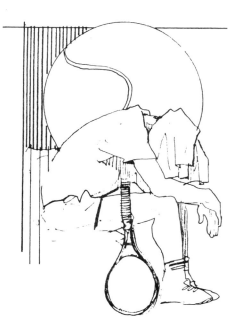

Practice beyond the point at which your interest lags is likely to be worse than a waste of time; for you will become careless and proceed to break down the improvement you have just attained by intense effort. Practice **does not necessarily** make perfect, but **correct** practice should enhance your game!

# DEVELOP TEAMWORK

Mathematically, one plus one equals two. Socially and psychologically one plus one can equal far **less** than two or considerably **more** than two. How often do you and an opponent go into a practice session with great hopes for satisfying progress? But the workout degenerates into a battle between the two of you rather than a well-planned, cooperative effort of mutual benefit to teammates. A fine shot by you is considered to be a loss of face by your opponent. A bystander hearing the comments would have to conclude that no one ever makes a fine shot. It's only that the opponent makes an inexcusable mistake! Bad sportsmanship becomes a habit and both of you suffer from inefficient use of your time.

You can profit immeasurably from cooperatively-planned practice in which you are gaining satisfaction from helping each other and are pleased with the progress made by either or both. For example, you and Joe are ready to work out. You would like some drill on return of service against a net rusher. That is fine with Joe since he could use some practice on serving and coming to the net. Joe agrees to begin with all serves to your forehand so that you can work on down-the-line passing shots. Joe also volleys deep to your forehand for more concentration on your forehand down the line. Joe doesn't move over to stand in front of your drives, but leaves enough of an opening to be passed on perfect shots close to the line. You both take pleasure in unusually good shots since you are helping the other while he helps himself. It isn't a "me agin' you" dog fight, but teamwork all the way.

The practice pattern is continued for a time and then may be varied or changed completely. You may hit all his forehands cross-court for a while. Joe may serve entirely to your backhand or to either side. You may change to rallying from the baseline for depth, emphasizing cross-court or down-the-line drives. The essential thing is that you **work together** for your mutual benefit. With this kind of mutually-planned practice, one plus one will add to more than two in progress and friendship.

# Tributes To Don Klotz, Teacher of Tennis and Life

# OLD COACHES NEVER DIE

by
Lawrence Tabak

Dr. Don Klotz, tennis analyst, coach, and innovator, likes to recall an incident that occurred some years ago at a national junior tournament. While looking over a draw he overheard a parent chuckling over his son's first round opponent.

"The kid's from someplace called Iowa City. How good could he be, anyway?"

Chances are that player learned that Iowa City was on the tennis map. No one will contest the fact that it was Klotz who put it there.

Don Klotz is 81 years old now. In November, 1983, his "kids" returned to Iowa City to honor their coach. They came from all over the country. They ranged from his first student, Art Andrews, who was the number one junior in the country in 1955, to one of his latest, a 14-year-old second-generation Klotz follower. A surprising number are still in tennis. Others, like Andrews, who is former Associate Dean of the University of Arizona Law School, aren't. No matter. Klotz is one of those rare coaches who seems to have the knack for making the lessons of tennis go far beyond the game. And the lessons continue. Although Klotz has been spreading the rumor of retirement for over a decade, on winter evenings he can still be found almost nightly at the indoor courts at the University of Iowa's Recreation Center.

He usually wears a white tennis jacket and a pair of gray cotton sweatpants. After unlocking the storage room he'll grab two baskets of balls and a racket and skip across the track between two joggers. As he strolls along next to the netting behind the six courts, a number of players wave or call out greetings. He sets his things behind the last court and crosses his arms, taking in all the action.

Then, with the sort of look he probably gave his first prospect in Iowa City in 1947, he notices a small figure in the corner, batting a ball against the wall. Without hurrying, Don makes his way toward that corner. The boy whacks the ball against the wall, swings wildly and manages another hit before it flies over his head. When he comes running back with the ball Don interrupts him.

"You won't mind," he says, smiling, "if an old man spoils your fun for a minute, will you?"

He then demonstrates a series of soft, consistent forehands.

"No harder than that. Just try to see how many times you can keep it going."

The boy takes his racket, thinks about it for a second, and then hits four in a row before missing. Both are obviously pleased.

After his hour lesson Don will stop again, this time on a court where two girls from one of the high school teams are punishing the ball. The two of them try to impress their spectator with even more aggressive shots. Klotz just shakes his head and motions them over.

"I just wanted to tell you two how nicely you hit the ball."

The two of them beam.

"However, hitting the ball nicely is not the object of the game."

The faces drop.

"Let me ask you a simple question. How many times will you hit the ball over the net in an average point? Six? Seven? Let me tell you. Four is pretty good tennis. How long were your rallies just now? Five was the record, and you weren't even serving. Half the shots in tennis are going to be serves and returns, so why drop the ball and hit it? Start your rallies with serves, and when you're practicing you should be keeping the ball going at least six times. Otherwise you're either overhitting or not concentrating. And you can't play tennis from that one little spot behind the baseline. You've got to learn to play the entire court, from the back fence to the net. So don't let the ball bounce twice. Go after those short balls! They're golden opportunities, not nuisances! You'll improve three times as fast."

The girls may or may not take the advice to heart, but over the years a great many players have. Among those returning that November to express their appreciation were Mona Schallau Guerrant, a U.S. top-tenner in 1975 and 1976; Chuck Darley, former number one at the University of California; and Steve Wilkinson, a 1983 NCAA Coach of the Year. For their 25th year reunion four members of Klotz's 1958 University of Iowa team were present. That team, composed almost entirely of home grown talent, without the benefit of a single tennis scholarship, won the Big Ten and went on to finish third in the nation.

But the reunion was more than a gathering of grateful champions. As the little boy hitting against the wall can attest, anyone capable of hitting a ball is a potential Klotz protegé.

When Don Klotz came to the University of Iowa in 1947 to begin work on his Ph.D., Iowa City was not exactly a haven for tennis. Iowa City had a population of 8,600, four good tennis courts and seven horrible ones.

During that first year Klotz noticed a couple of neighborhood boys hitting a bare ball around out in the street.

"I thought it might be interesting," Don explains years later, "to see just how far a couple of kids like that could go."

The older brother, Jim, now a professor of engineering at the University of Iowa, became a Missouri Valley champion. His younger brother, Art Andrews, was the leader of that 1958 Big Ten championship team.

Jim Andrews sums up the role that Don had in his life. "As far as the tennis, he made it all possible. Even a small thing like balls. I still don't know where all of those balls came from. He would go around to businesses and get money to send us to tournaments. There was no way we could have afforded entry fees, let alone the transportation to Kalamazoo or St. Louis. I grew up without a father, and Don filled that sort of need for Art and me. You can't imagine a better person you'd want to have around growing kids. His consideration, his immense patience, just the basic decency of the man. We were extremely lucky to have Don around."

At the banquet a series of speakers reminisced about their days in the Iowa City program. Tellingly, most of the memories had little to do with the learning of style or technique. Mona Guerrant remembered how Klotz, after seeing her play for the first time, had "borrowed" her old racket and restrung it for her. Guerrant also recalled how she had made the mistake, at eleven, of tossing a candy wrapper out of the car window. "Does anyone else remember that 45 minute lecture?" she asked, adding, "I haven't littered since."

Chuck Darley recalled the excitement he felt as a young beginner when he received a ribbon for his first successful set of volleys. Klotz is known as the originator of the "volley method" of teaching, where students start close to the net and move progressively further away, adding more and more swing as they go. Darley obviously learned the lesson well. Observers of the game still cite him as one of the best volleyers they have ever seen.

Darley, a teaching pro with a Ph.D. in clinical psychology, also recalled the "magical" aura that tennis had for him under Klotz. One of the reasons that so many felt compelled to organize and attend the reunion was what Darley described as the sense of family. "I'll never forget the way the older players felt an obligation to the younger ones, to pass on their knowledge and experience."

Art Andrews admits that "the junior program was too good to be true. He was constantly fighting to get us space at the University Field House. We'd practice hitting on a handball court, or on chalked lines on the dirt of the ROTC section. Plus we had the courts on the basketball courts where I had to face Bob Potthast's serve, my back against the wall. And then there was Don's 'junior fund.' I think we all know where a lot of that came from—Don's pocket. And it was more than tennis. He had a great influence on how we thought about ourselves, on becoming independent, and how it was possible to reach our potentials in whatever we did. To those of us he coached, he was more than a great coach. He was a great man."

Klotz's influence in tennis reached well beyond Iowa City. Many of the secrets of his success were revealed in a series of articles that began appearing in World Tennis in the 1950's. His "Purposeful Practice" series shook up an entire venerated, if ill-considered, tradition of tennis training.

He felt an obligation, as coach of the University team, to spread the word of tennis around the state. With a couple of his top young players he caravanned across Iowa. Steve Wilkinson remembers one of those tours.

"I was about nine years old when I went to see Don's clinic. I watched Art Andrews play and was amazed. I never knew anyone could play tennis like that. I remember that when Dr. Klotz saw me hitting, he told me that I had a lot of potential, that I could be a pretty good player if I wanted."

Klotz was the only major college coach to recruit Wilkinson out of Sioux City High. Four years later Wilkinson was a point away from taking the Big Ten championship away from Marty Riessen.

"Don taught us to admire the marvelous human body and to wonder at the computer that was on our shoulders. We learned a great deal about tennis, but more importantly, he taught me what it meant to be a teacher, and the joy that is possible in teaching. I call my summer tennis camps 'Tennis and Life Camps.' That tells a great deal of the story," Wilkinson said.

Throughout the evening Don sat between the podium and his wife Vivian, laughing at the anecdotes, shifting uncomfortably at the accolades. When it was his turn to speak Klotz stood for a few seconds, distractedly wiping a hand across his brow, and then briefly uttered his thanks.

Klotz's friends and former students had presented him with a gift—a week's worth of trout fishing at a Wisconsin resort.

As Don stood uncomfortably in front of the podium, it was easy to picture him in a plaid shirt and waders, casting the fly with a swift, efficient flick. The sort of cast that takes years and years to perfect. It would be hard to imagine a better person to show you just how it's done.

July, 1987
Princeton, New Jersey

Reprinted with permission of **Addvantage Magazine** March/April, 1984.

## "THANK YOU, DR. KLOTZ"
by
Steve Wilkinson

It was some 36 years ago that you, Art Andrews, and several other Iowa Citians journeyed to that remote corner of the state where Sioux City is located. What a day that was for me! I didn't know tennis could be played that well. You spent all afternoon helping anyone who was willing to be helped. Then, near the end of the day, when only the most dedicated still remained, you told me that I had potential! I was elated!! THE Dr. Klotz thought there was a future in tennis for me, a gangly boy nine years old. That afternoon must have kept me going for another few years.

Immediately following my senior year in high school, you stepped into my life again. I was prepared to attend a small college where I would be able to play basketball as well as tennis, while pursuing a good education. I never dreamed that I would be wanted on a state university team which had just won the Big Ten and had finished among the top three teams in the NCAA. Again, you saw something in me. You convinced me to attend the University of Iowa. Since that time I have often heard you say, "Any fool can see the seeds in the apple. It takes God to see the apple in the seed." I thank you for your perceptiveness. I have grown, nurtured by your vision of what I could become.

I can remember you sitting there beside the Field House basketball floor that became a tennis court through the addition of two sawhorses, a block and tackle, elastic lines, and your ingenuity. You had your clipboard in your lap, and you charted my matches.

Being a competitive person, I wanted so much for my statistics to look good. I longed for a high percentage of winners compared to unforced errors. I hoped for your praise on my resourcefulness—how I had used my head, tried something different when my opponent was hot or I was cold, and kept trying to the end. In the process of this training under you, I came to believe that there was a way to beat everyone.

Dr. Klotz, you were always amazed at how people with such pretty strokes often got so little out of their game. You talked with such pride about Joe Martin, a dedicated competitor from Keokuk, who had won the Big Ten without a strong backhand. I realize now that it was not by accident that I heard so much about Joe. I was another young player without a backhand, but you never caused me to worry about it. I realize now that I could have spent my years at Iowa trying to master an inadequate backhand, and would never have learned how competitive I could be. You taught me that no points are awarded for form. Therefore, it never occurred to me that I shouldn't be able to beat any master of form who did not understand the subtleties of percentage tennis.

What I learned on the court from you was monumental, but small by comparison to the lessons about life which you shared continually. I remember our long road trips, the times I sat on the couch in your office while you strung our rackets, and the frequent visits to your home, which always included some of Vivian's delicious home made cooking. Both what you said and did was an inspiration for me. Through your example, I learned the joy of being a teacher, of taking time to help anyone who was willing to listen, of serving others with no thought of monetary reimbursement. As a staff member at the University of Iowa, you thought it was your responsibility to promote tennis throughout the state, without pay.

Dr. Klotz, you were always a minister disguised in tennis clothing. You came to teach tennis, but you always taught much more. You taught us to marvel at our wonderful God-given bodies, to trust that magnificent computer which had been placed on our shoulders, to enjoy ourselves and others as we played. We learned your lessons quickly, because you were so enthusiastic about us. You had a way of perceiving the beauty in ourselves that we so often overlooked.

Dr. Klotz, you taught me what it meant to be a teacher. I watched you teach, hour after hour. I saw the looks of surprise and then delight when you would take time to help any beginner. I saw you win their confidence with words of praise that had them smiling like Cheshire cats within a minute or two. They didn't realize how good they were—until you pointed it out. Then I watched you skillfully slip in a couple of observations that just might help them play even better. They were usually amazed at how quickly those suggestions led to improvements in their game. As I watched you help them, I was amazed also. Teaching was so easy, so rewarding, so much fun!

You gave us the Volley Method of teaching tennis, and I have used it ever since. Why not start with the volley? No one else did at the time, but that certainly did not bother you. Why not start with something that was simple and then progress to the more difficult? What could be easier than holding the racket in front of you as you stood close to the net and blocking the ball back? As soon as your students could do that, you were immediately on to something else that was slightly more difficult. You continually sang their praises. You could hear your students thinking, "Hey, this isn't so hard, after all!" Next, you had them playing little games from the service line and learning the basics of strategy, often in their first lesson. It was amazing how much could be accomplished in a short time when you used the athletic skills your students possessed naturally, implemented a progression method which helped you avoid the dangers of over-teaching, and added generous amounts of praise and enthusiasm.

Dr. Klotz, you were an innovator, a man so far ahead of his time that many could not understand or agree with you. It was preposterous that you should suggest ping pong scoring, tie breakers, and other modifications in the scoring system. That was accepted only 15 years later. I chuckle when "new" developments come into the tennis teaching profession—inner tennis, progression instruction, a strategic framework for teaching. I was learning similar insights from you over 25 years ago!

Many of your insights make so much sense, but still most players resist with a passion. What could make more sense than starting practice rallies with a serve instead of a groundstroke? After all, 65% of all strokes hit are serve and service returns. Why allow the ball to bounce twice in a practice? Practice or adjusting to the ball is lost. Why hit the ball to each other in the middle of the court during practice, when you would never want to do that in a match? These and a thousand other questions prodded us to question our conventional way of doing things, even if they did not cause us to change. What you were telling us, Dr. Klotz, simply was not the customary way of doing things. Traditions have been hard for most of us to break, even when undermined by your perceptive observations.

Recently I have realized how nice it would be if more people could benefit from your wisdom. What a joy it has been, going through your closets and files, finding articles which in some cases have gathered dust for over twenty years! I, with the assistance of Jane Latourette, have edited many of your articles on tennis teaching and assembled them into six chapters. I have benefited immensely from this labor of love. If others, by reading this volume, share only a portion of what I have experienced, they will be richly blessed.

July, 1987
Gustavus Adolphus College
St. Peter, Minnesota

# DON KLOTZ
# A Brief Biography
by
Jane Latourette

Don was born on August 19, 1905, on a farm near Independence, Iowa. By the age of eight he was playing tennis on an improvised court in the barnyard. After lettering in basketball, baseball, track and tennis in high school, Don continued his emphasis on sports in undergraduate study at the University of Northern Iowa (1931-34). The fact that he minored in math, physics, biology, English and history indicated the breadth of his preparation for his life of service.

After seven years of teaching and coaching in the public schools and doing graduate work in the summers, Don earned his M.S. Degree in 1941 at the University of Iowa. His Ph.D. work was interrupted by three and a half years in the Armed Forces, and in the spring of 1946 he returned to study and teach. In May, 1947, he was named Head Tennis Coach and completed his Ph.D. in Physical Education in 1948.

With great ingenuity, Don set up tennis courts for year-round play in the huge Field House, and he began developing his special outdoor, subsurface-watered, clay courts (for which he gained a patent

in the 1960's). With this extensive "laboratory" in place for training tennis players, Don began a junior program along with the varsity plan.

In a little over two years, Jamie Andrews won the Missouri Valley 15-under Singles and Doubles Championship and made it to the finals for the National 15-under Indoor Championships. From then on, Don had from one to three Iowa City juniors in the national rankings each year. Brother Art Andrews won the National Indoor 15 Singles and Doubles Championships in 1952 and was ranked No. 1 in the nation, Junior Singles and Doubles in 1955. Mona Schallau Guerrant was another protegé of Don's during her early teens, and went on into national and international competition, with high rankings in both doubles and singles.

At the same time, Don's varsity teams were breaking every record the school had previously set: Big Ten Champions in 1958; third in the NCAA that year; fourth and ninth in subsequent years. In addition, from 1950 on into the 80's, Don wrote numerous articles for tennis magazines. Using another mode for letting many people benefit from his discoveries about learning to play tennis, Don spent his summers traveling all over the midwest (and more widely) with some varsity players, conducting clinics, finding local leaders, setting up tennis programs. Inspiring young players was his mission.

His individual awards have been numerous:

Honorary Member, Iowa City Junior Chamber of Commerce, 1960

U.S.L.T.A Umpire's Association, Life Membership, 1963

World Tennis Marlboro Award, 1964

University of Iowa plaque, "For dedication to sports, excellence in teaching, coaching and human relations," 1970

Iowa Tennis Hall of Fame, 1974

National Honorary Member, USPTA, 1978

Plaque for Contributions to Tennis by former varsity players, 1983

University of Iowa named its varsity courts The Donald D. Klotz Tennis Center, 1987.

United States Tennis Association, Inc. plaque, "In special recognition for a lifetime of service to the game of tennis," 1987

Photos clockwise from upper left:

Dr. Donald D. Klotz

Outstanding Juniors, 1949. Kneeling from left to right: Jamie Andrews, Suzy Hamilton, Dr. Klotz, Art Andrews, Ruthie Ashton.

Dr. Klotz demonstrates volley. Standing from left to right: Dargy Hamilton, Mona Schallau, Terry Paul, Nathan Chapman.

Art Andrews, 1958, captain of The University of Iowa Big Ten Championship Tennis Team and No. 1 singles and doubles National Champion.

University of Iowa Tennis Team, 1958, Big Ten Champions. Standing from left to right: John Stoy, No. 6; Joe Martin, No. 3; Coach Don Klotz; Art Andrews, No. 1; Bob Potthast, No. 2. Kneeling from left to right; Don Middlebrook, No. 4; Bill Voxman, No. 5.

# Chronological Bibliography of Published Articles
by
Dr. Donald D. Klotz

"The Beginner May Know More Tennis Than You Think," **State Journal of Health, Physical Education & Recreation**. March, 1952.

**Outline for the USLTA on the Iowa Junior Tennis Program**. April, 1953.

"Coach, What's Wrong with My Serve?" **The Racquet**. March, 1953.

"Is Drinking such a Crime?—Smart Players Know Better," **International Tennis News**. 1953

"There Is No Substitute for Leadership," **International Tennis News**. Nov., 1953.

"Begin Your Practice Rallies with a Serve," **The Racquet**. Aug., 1953.

"The Art of Concentration," **World Tennis**. Jan., 1954.

"How Much Should Drives Clear the Net?" **World Tennis**. April, 1954.

"How Waterloo Revived Tennis," by Dave Archie and Don Klotz, **The Iowan**. Aug.-Sept., 1954. (Photographs by George Black)

"Steady, Heady Tennis," **World Tennis**. Nov., 1954.

"Practice Does Not Make Perfect," **World Tennis**. Aug., 1954. (Reprinted in **Scholastic Coach**, 1955.)

"Forcing Psychologically in Tennis," **World Tennis**. Jan., 1955.

"Forcing Psychologically in Tennis, No. 2," **World Tennis**. Feb., 1955.

"The Art of Learning Tennis," **World Tennis**. April, 1955.

"Fundamentals of Habit Change," **World Tennis**. May, 1955.

"Three Common Faults in Match Play," **World Tennis**. Dec., 1955.

"Two Guides for Performance in Match Play," **World Tennis**. Jan., 1956.

"Purposeful Practice, No. 1: The Warm-Up," **World Tennis**. April, 1956.

"Purposeful Practice, No. 2: Making the Practice Pattern More Fruitful," **World Tennis**. May, 1956.

"Good Tennis Is Simple," **Scholastic Coach**. March, 1956.

"A Simple Serve for Beginners," **Scholastic Coach**. April, 1956.

"The Pro Questionnaire," **World Tennis**. Dec., 1956. (A series of questions put to ten tennis professionals.)

"Defense: Tennis's Neglected Art," **Scholastic Coach**. March, 1957.

"Temporary Marking for an Indoor Tennis Court," **World Tennis**. Jan., 1957.

"A Simple and Effective Scoreboard for Tennis," **World Tennis**. Feb., 1958.

"Tradition or Common Sense?" **World Tennis**. June, 1959.

"Tennis Tips," **World Tennis**. Feb., 1962.

"The Volley Method," **World Tennis**. March, 1962.

"Volley Practice," **World Tennis**. April, 1962.

"Percentage Play," **World Tennis**. May, 1962.

"Steady Play," **World Tennis**. June, 1962.

"Teamwork in Practice," **World Tennis**. July, 1962.

"Focus Your Efforts," **World Tennis**. Dec., 1962.

"Competitive Limits" in "Letters to the Editor," **World Tennis**. Feb., 1964.

"Developing Strategy," **World Tennis**. June, 1969.

"Employing Instinct in Learning" **World Tennis**. Sept., 1972.

"A Better Way to Practice," **World Tennis**. Jan., 1973.

"Groundstrokes vs. Volley Reflexes," **World Tennis**. May, 1973.

"No Second Bounces," **World Tennis**. Jan., 1974.

"Trigger Your Concentration," **World Tennis**. April, 1974.

"Take Advantage of the High Bounce, **World Tennis**. Oct., 1977.

"When You Are Out of Position," **World Tennis**. May, 1978.

"One Step at a Time," **World Tennis**. July, 1978.

"Changing Strokes Is Risky Business," **USPTA-ADD**. July-Aug., 1982.

"Five Limits on Strokes," **USPTA-ADD**. Sept.-Oct., 1983.

"Two-handed Forehand for Beginners," **USPTA-ADD**. Nov.-Dec., 1983.

"The Doctor Answers the Professor," **USPTA-ADD**. March-April, 1984.

"Sneak Up on Your Opponent," **USPTA-ADD**. Sept.-Oct., 1985.

"Take Advantage of That Pesky High Bounce," **USPTA-ADD**. Jan.-Feb., 1986.